A Question of Mercy

DAVID RABE

A QUESTION OF MERCY

Based on the essay by Richard Selzer

Grove Press/New York

"A Question of Mercy" by Richard Selzer originally appeared in *The New York Times Magazine* on September 22, 1991, and is included in Richard Selzer's *Down from Troy* (New York: William Morrow and Company, Inc., 1992).

Published simultaneously in Canada
Printed in the United States of America

FIRST EDITION

Library of Congress Cataloging-in-Publication Data

Rabe, David.
    A question of mercy : a play / by David Rabe : based on the essay
by Richard Selzer.
        p.   cm.
    ISBN 0-8021-3549-8
    1. AIDS (Disease)—Patients—United States—Drama.   2. Euthanasia—
United States—Drama.   3. Gay men—United States—Drama.
    I. Selzer, Richard, 1928– . II. Title.
PS3568.A23Q47   1998
812'.54—dc21   97-40046

DESIGN BY LAURA HAMMOND HOUGH

Grove Press
841 Broadway
New York, NY 10003

98 99 00 01 10 9 8 7 6 5 4 3 2 1

For Ruth McCormick Rabe

A *Question of Mercy* premiered at New York Theatre Workshop on February 7, 1997, under the direction of Douglas Hughes with the following cast:

Dr. Robert Chapman: Zach Grenier
Thomas: Stephen Spinella
Anthony: Juan Carlos Hernandez
Susanah: Veanne Cox
Doorman (Eddie): Michael Kell
Others: Doc Dougherty and Christopher Burns

CHARACTERS

Dr. Robert Chapman
Thomas
Anthony
Susanah
Doorman (Eddie)
Cops
Hospital Attendants

ACT ONE

The set is a raised, raked platform surrounded by a ground-level alley that runs along stage right and left and across the front. The backdrop is abstract. Perhaps it suggests an urban skyline. Downstage left on the ground-floor ramp stands a table with a phone on it.
There is music and a dreamy kind of light on DR. ROBERT CHAPMAN *as he enters upstage left. He's in his forties, tall, and he walks down toward the table and chair. He wears an overcoat, which he unbuttons, then removes. He looks out to the audience, taking them in. He speaks as if making a formal presentation on a supremely important issue.*

DR. CHAPMAN: This overcoat—my overcoat was given to me ten—no. He's twenty-three now and he was . . . so it's . . . my overcoat is fifteen years old. It was a Christmas gift from my nephew. I'm sure it was really my sister who purchased it. But my nephew was the bearer, his little face a bright bulb above the festive package as he raced across the room. (*Slightly puzzled, but still grand, he continues.*) I don't know why I'm saying this. But I wear it—the overcoat—when I go out in cold weather. (*With the overcoat in one hand, he turns to a pair of pajamas on the chair.*) These are my pajamas. (*Grabbing them up.*) At night, I wear them. They provide a kind of consoling formality. (*He holds the pajamas in one hand, the overcoat in the other, both arms outstretched as he weighs*

the garments, his arms shifting like scales.) The boundary, the demarcation between waking and sleeping, between thought and dreams, benefits, I believe, from such an acknowledgment—a gesture of respect, of emphasis, I think.
The phone rings. The backdrop holds a projection, narrow and clear: JANUARY 9, 1990.
    DR. CHAPMAN *picks up a nearby leather-bound appointment book and looks at it. The phone rings again. He looks at it, grabs it up.*

DR. CHAPMAN: Hello?

VOICE: Dr. Robert Chapman?

DR. CHAPMAN: Who is this?

VOICE: This is Thomas Ames. We met at the—at the fundraiser for—

DR. CHAPMAN: Oh, yes, of course.

THOMAS: Do you remember me?
    Now on the stage right area, lights find THOMAS AMES, *standing alone with a phone in his hand. He is handsome, slim, in his thirties.*

DR. CHAPMAN: Yes, yes, at the Levines' house. For the Franklin Coalition.

THOMAS: I was wondering if we might—I hate to intrude, but would you have time for a cup of coffee in the next few days? I wouldn't take much of your time. But there's something I need to discuss, and the phone doesn't seem quite appropriate, but—

DR. CHAPMAN: Well, I'm actually quite busy.

THOMAS: I mean, I could do it on the phone, but—

DR. CHAPMAN: What am I saying? Of course. A cup of coffee? Tomorrow morning?

THOMAS: I'll come to your neighborhood. Just name a place.

DR. CHAPMAN: Well, the Beacon is quite close by.

THOMAS: Oh, yes. Of course. I know it. What time shall we say?

DR. CHAPMAN: Is ten good for you?

THOMAS: Fine. Perfect. I'll see you then.

DR. CHAPMAN: I look forward to it.
DR. CHAPMAN stands looking at the phone in his hand.

THOMAS *(as the lights take him out of view)*: Good-bye.
On the screen above and behind DR. CHAPMAN is projected: JANUARY 10, 1990.

DR. CHAPMAN *(leafing through pages in his appointment book)*: January eighth, ninth, tenth, eleventh. They flow by. A haze. A confident haze. A sense of will. Intention. My life. I will do this. I will do that.
As the lights come up on the stage right area, we see THOMAS seated at a table with a flowered tablecloth spread over it. A pot of coffee stands on the table; there are two cups and saucers and some Danish on a plate, awaiting DR. CHAPMAN.

THOMAS (*waving toward* DR. CHAPMAN): Dr. Chapman! Here! Here I am!

DR. CHAPMAN *waves back and heads to the table.*

DR. CHAPMAN: Thomas, hello. Sorry I'm late.

THOMAS: No, no, I arrived a little early, I think.

DR. CHAPMAN: How are you? Busy, I bet.

THOMAS: Oh, yes. (*Gesturing toward the coffee, the plate of Danish.*) I took the liberty of ordering coffee and some Danish for us. I hope that's all right.

DR. CHAPMAN: As long as there's blueberry. Have you seen the Levines' recently? (*He seeks amid the Danish.*)

THOMAS: No, no—not for some weeks now.

DR. CHAPMAN: I haven't either. I should call them.
For a slight uneasy pause, they look around.

THOMAS: This is awkward—isn't it. I'm sorry.

DR. CHAPMAN: And slightly mysterious, I must admit.

THOMAS: I'm . . . how shall I put this? It's just that I felt in our conversation at the Levines' that day—we ended up in a small group, do you remember?

DR. CHAPMAN: Yes.

THOMAS: I mean, I don't even remember the subject under discussion, but what I do remember emphatically was that something in your manner—it could have been something you said, an opinion you expressed. Anyway, what happened is I came away with the impression that you would be sympathetic to the issue about which— the issue that prompted my call—and of course I could be wrong, but—goodness, I don't feel I'm handling this at all well, but you're a doctor, right?

Dr. Chapman: Well, I was. I don't practice anymore, if you're—

Thomas: But you're still licensed, aren't you? You are still licensed.

Dr. Chapman: So this is a medical matter?

Thomas: Well, yes.

Dr. Chapman: Are you ill?

Thomas: It's not me. It's a friend of mine. Though I'm certainly involved. A dear friend. It's AIDS. He has AIDS.

Dr. Chapman: I see.

Thomas: He was HIV for so many years, it all seemed— everything just seemed—it seemed . . . ! We were lulled into a kind of expectation that this almost normal health would just simply go on and on, but then it all changed. Seven months ago we went from our lives into—into— a nightmare.

Dr. Chapman: I'm not a doctor anymore. I don't treat patients.

Thomas: Well, I mean, treatment is not exactly what we were—what he and I were discussing.

DR. CHAPMAN: Well, treatment is what I administered as a doctor.

THOMAS: He thought you might—that you might be willing—he wanted me to ask if you would be willing to consider helping him.

DR. CHAPMAN: Help him in what way?

THOMAS: Well, if you would be willing to intervene on his behalf.

DR. CHAPMAN: I don't understand, Thomas.

THOMAS: If you would intervene.

DR. CHAPMAN: I'm not practicing medicine at the moment, Thomas. (*Glancing at his watch.*) And I'm afraid I took you quite literally regarding the time we'd need for this cup of coffee. I have to get back to my office.
As DR. CHAPMAN *rises:*

THOMAS: Well . . . I see. . . .

DR. CHAPMAN: I'm sorry about your friend. I wish you the best of luck.
As DR. CHAPMAN *turns and leaves,* THOMAS *watches him. The lights fade on* THOMAS *and focus on* DR. CHAPMAN, *who steps downstage, facing out. He opens his appointment book. Projected on the screen is: JANUARY 11, 1990.*

DR. CHAPMAN: It says in my appointment calendar that later today I have to go to the dentist for a checkup. He has a new nurse whom I find annoying, but—well—it says, "Tomatoes. Onions. Peppers. Et cetera." The "et cetera" meaning additional vegetables. (*He turns a page.*) I've enrolled in a cooking course at the . . . well . . . I might as well admit it: the Learning Annex. (*He smiles.*) The first class is tonight. And the truth is, I'm looking forward to it.

The phone starts to ring. Annoyed, DR. CHAPMAN *looks at it.*

DR. CHAPMAN: How it intrudes. The ringing telephone and the course of our thoughts, the flow of our own intentions is cut off. We answer it, and most of the time it's a minor tug, easily incorporated. And if we didn't answer, might the caller just disappear? Might he never call back? (*Picking up phone.*) Hello!

The lights come up on THOMAS *and* ANTHONY *center stage in a fragmentary depiction of their apartment. They sit beside each other on the couch.* THOMAS *talks on the phone.* ANTHONY *sits on the couch. A short, delicate man with black, close-cropped hair, a neatly trimmed black beard,* ANTHONY *is also in his thirties; although extremely pale, he is surprisingly unwasted.*

THOMAS: Dr. Chapman. This is Thomas Ames. I'm sorry to bother you, but my friend—the friend I mentioned—he insisted that I call you. When I described our conversation in the coffee shop, he felt I had been too oblique.

As THOMAS *talks,* DR. CHAPMAN, *phone to ear, listens, idly leafing through pages in a cookbook.*

THOMAS: He's quite annoyed with me because he feels I failed—that, given my annoyingly inveterate allegiance to discretion, I failed to convey the real nature of what I

was saying. Or trying to say. He said I must speak to you
again, and I must be candid.

DR. CHAPMAN: I think I understood you, Thomas.

THOMAS: I know. I know you did. This is really more about
him and me—our relationship, but he has things he feels
I must say directly before he can believe that we've made
our best effort in your direction. If you could indulge us
just for a, for a—they're tormenting him, these things,
and he has enough tormenting him. So if you could indulge me for just a moment.

DR. CHAPMAN: I was about to go out, but I have a minute.

THOMAS: Thank you, thank you. He wanted me to tell you that
he's my lover—that's the first thing he wanted to make
absolutely clear—that he is not just some casual acquain-
tance or even just a friend, but we live together, have
lived together for seven and a half years. And the second
thing is that he's suffering terribly—it's really pretty far
along and it was in the midst of his suffering that your
name came up. That it was not casual, because it wasn't.
Nothing about this is casual. I guess I told him about
meeting you at the Levines' and he asked me to call you.
This is the first call I'm talking about—the one the other
day.

DR. CHAPMAN: Yes.

THOMAS: But now, as far as this call is concerned, he's demanding that I make it unequivocal—that I make it totally
clear that when I said "intervene," if you recall—well,

he found that just infuriatingly vague on my part because what he wants is to die. He's almost always in pain, and he wants to die. And that's what he sent me to ask you. It's what I meant by "intervene," which I thought you understood—but he says, how could you possibly? So he has insisted that I call and ask you if you would help him commit suicide.

DR. CHAPMAN *closes the book and sets it on the table.*

THOMAS: He wants you to help him die.

ANTHONY: While I still have the strength to do it.

THOMAS (*to Anthony*): What?

ANTHONY: While I still have the strength to—

THOMAS (*into phone*): While he still has the strength to do it.

DR. CHAPMAN: I'm sorry, but that's not possible.

THOMAS: Oh.

DR. CHAPMAN: That's all. I'm sorry.

THOMAS: This is a horrible disease, Doctor. Have you seen anyone with it?

DR. CHAPMAN: My training, my thinking, my philosophy have all been directed toward the preservation of life—that's what I did, what I wanted to do, and—

ANTHONY: Ask him if he thinks a doctor's purpose is to lessen misfortune or to prolong it as long as possible.

THOMAS (*into the phone*): Wait a minute. Wait a minute.

DR. CHAPMAN: What? Are you talking to me?

THOMAS (*to Anthony*): He says he can't help us, Anthony.

ANTHONY: But why?

THOMAS: His philosophy. His training. His thinking—I don't know.

ANTHONY: What did he say?

THOMAS (*into phone*): Dr. Chapman. He needs help. He's asking for help to lessen his pain. Isn't that your task, your oath as a doctor?

DR. CHAPMAN: No. In fact, it isn't. There are laws, Thomas, there's society. I'm not a barbarian.

THOMAS: But to let him suffer like this—that's the very word he uses about it. To let him suffer like this is the act of a barbarian!

ANTHONY: Don't insult him. Why are you insulting him?

THOMAS: I'm not.

ANTHONY: You just called him a "barbarian."

THOMAS: Well, he—I—

ANTHONY: Apologize.

THOMAS (*into phone*): Could you come and talk to us about it all, at least? I think, if you did that, we might be able to see it your way.

ANTHONY: I know what I want, Thomas.

THOMAS (*into phone*): Could you at least do that, Dr. Chapman? Visit us. If you could counsel us. If you could talk to him. I don't really want him to do it either. Perhaps that's all he needs—all we both need—someone to talk to us from your perspective. If you spent some time with Anthony and me, so that—

ANTHONY: Let me talk to him.

THOMAS: Anthony wants to talk to you. All right?

DR. CHAPMAN: Yes.

THOMAS: All right.
    ANTHONY *takes the phone.*

ANTHONY: I implore you, Dr. Chapman. I implore you. Do you hear me?

DR. CHAPMAN (*lowering phone, looking out*): "I implore you," he says. "I implore you." And I feel I must meet him. I wanted to meet—no. To see him. (*Looking at the phone.*) It's startling the way his voice reaches out through this object in my—

ANTHONY: Dr. Chapman?

DR. CHAPMAN (*into phone*): All right. Tuesday. (*He hangs up.*) *Lights sweep* THOMAS *and* ANTHONY *away.* DR. CHAPMAN *stands alone. Music plays in the background.*

DR. CHAPMAN (*putting on his coat, his scarf*): Ambivalence is an equal pull in opposing directions, and so each year I renew the license that allows me to prescribe narcotics. The drugs he implored me to provide are drugs I can easily acquire. Because his desire is not a stranger to me. I mean, I've thought that I might want to prescribe such pills to myself someday. To relieve pain or to end my own life, should the need arise. I've thought of it. I've thought of it often, but it's always been slightly distanced. A principled matter. A theoretical option. But then the pain in his voice burst through, and I thought, My life is good. I'm healthy. More or less happy. If I would do it for myself, why not for him?
The lights take DR. CHAPMAN *away, and projected on the screen is: JANUARY 16, 1990.*

On the stage left corner of the ramp, a DOORMAN *clutches a package wrapped in brown paper as he talks on the intercom phone.*

DOORMAN: Sure, Mrs. Waxman, I'll make certain Tommy knows to hold this for UPS in the morning. When he comes on at midnight, I will leave no doubt about the importance of this package. And he will convey that importance to Edgar first thing in the morning.
As DR. CHAPMAN *approaches, crossing along the downstage ramp:*

DOORMAN: No, no. No problem, Mrs. Waxman. Listen, could you hold on a second? Just a second.
THE DOORMAN *puts his hand over the phone and steps in front of* DR. CHAPMAN.

DOORMAN: Dr. Chapman?

DR. CHAPMAN: What?

DOORMAN: It's me, Dr. Chapman. Eddie Ruggerio, remember me? (*As* DR. CHAPMAN *stares.*) You took my gallbladder out!

DR. CHAPMAN: Oh, yes. Eddie. Eddie! My goodness. Hello! *As they shake hands:*

DOORMAN: I compliment you all the time, Dr. Chapman.

DR. CHAPMAN: Eddie. How are you?

DOORMAN: I tell everybody you did an incredible job, because you did. What else am I gonna tell them, right? The scar has all but disappeared. Look. (*Pulling his jacket open, his shirt up, showing the faint scar.*) I gotta point it out to people or nobody sees it. Do you see it? *He points and* DR. CHAPMAN *looks.*

DOORMAN: I could be in a beauty pageant. Right? If I was a beauty. (*Back to the intercom phone.*) Mrs. Waxman— that doctor I'm always telling you about. He's here. . . . Right! . . . Yes! The gallbladder Svengali. He's right here standing in front of me. He's one great surgeon, Mrs. Waxman, if you need anything. . . . That's right.

DR. CHAPMAN: Actually, I'm not practicing at the moment, Eddie.

DOORMAN: What? You've retired? Oh, no. No, no. How could you? Look at you, you're in the prime of life, Dr. Chapman.

DR. CHAPMAN: It's sad but true, Eddie, I guess.

DOORMAN (*into phone*): He's retired, Mrs. Waxman. . . . Yes, it is too bad. That's just what I said. . . . He's the best, though. The best ever. (*Returning to* DR. CHAPMAN.) I'm sorry. You have friends here?

DR. CHAPMAN: Thomas Ames is a friend of mine.

DOORMAN: Oh, yes. Ten-C. Well, great to see you.

DR. CHAPMAN: Great to see you, Eddie.
As DR. CHAPMAN *moves along the ramp to the upstage left corner of the raked platform, the* DOORMAN *talks on the phone.*

DOORMAN: He's a miracle man, Mrs. Waxman. I mean, next time you're down here, I'll show you the scar. But it's nothing. A wrinkle.
A doorbell rings. In their apartment, THOMAS *moves to the door.* ANTHONY *waits on the couch.*

DOORMAN (*into phone*): And he did it with a knife, Mrs. Waxman. With a knife.
As the lights sweep EDDIE *away,* DR. CHAPMAN *steps up onto the raked platform.*

THOMAS: Hello.

DR. CHAPMAN: Hello, Thomas.

THOMAS: Come in, come in. Is it snowing? It's still snowing.

DR. CHAPMAN: Very lightly, but—yes.

THOMAS: Let me take your coat.
THOMAS *takes* DR. CHAPMAN's *coat and lays it over a chair upstage.*

DR. CHAPMAN: Do you know—just now, the doorman—it was such a coincidence.

THOMAS: Eddie?

DR. CHAPMAN: He was a former patient of mine.

THOMAS: Really.

DR. CHAPMAN: I took his gallbladder out.
THOMAS *has moved to stand behind* ANTHONY, *who sits on an invalid's cushion on the couch. He presents* AN-THONY *to* DR. CHAPMAN.

THOMAS: This is Anthony. It's still snowing, Anthony. Anthony loves the snow. He's from Colombia.

ANTHONY: But please don't conclude I spent my childhood following burros up mountains looking for coffee beans.
As ANTHONY, *grinning, half rises, extends his hand:*

DR. CHAPMAN: No, no. Please. Don't get up.
They shake hands; ANTHONY *settles back on his cushion.*

ANTHONY: I find a certain magic in the snow—as if it is not quite real. I saw very little snow.

DR. CHAPMAN: Except in the mountains.

ANTHONY: Well, yes, the mountains. But I didn't grow up in the mountains.

*From offstage, a teakettle whistles. On the coffee table
in front of the couch sits a plate of cookies.*

THOMAS: I was just brewing some tea. Would you like some tea?

DR. CHAPMAN: Yes, that would be fine.

THOMAS: I have herbal and regular.

ANTHONY: Many kinds of herbal tea.

DR. CHAPMAN: I think I'd like regular.
    As THOMAS *darts into the kitchen,* ANTHONY *pats the
    couch for* DR. CHAPMAN *to sit beside him.*

ANTHONY: Would you like a cookie? They're chocolate chip.
    (*He picks up a cookie.*) Thomas made them today.
    They're fresh.

DR. CHAPMAN: Thank you.
    DR. CHAPMAN *selects a cookie and takes a bite. As* AN-
    THONY *waits awkwardly, he surveys the apartment.*

ANTHONY: We've been here five years.

DR. CHAPMAN: It's a beautiful apartment.

ANTHONY: So many things we had to—not fix, but adapt to our
    own taste after moving in. And there was never enough
    money. Our tastes have blended very nicely, don't you
    think?

DR. CHAPMAN: It appears the work of a single mind.
    THOMAS *comes hurrying in with a tray bearing a teapot,
    milk, sugar, and Equal. He pours tea for* DR. CHAPMAN.

ANTHONY: He likes the decor, Thomas.

DR. CHAPMAN (*rising, pacing, surveying*): You must have had a decorator help you.

ANTHONY: No, no, this is our own—our mutual expression.

THOMAS: Sugar?

DR. CHAPMAN: Yes. And a little milk.

THOMAS (*starting to pour*): Say when? Personally, I like—(*Stopping.*) You could pour it yourself if you preferred.

DR. CHAPMAN: Well . . . no. You go right ahead.

THOMAS: We have Equal, if you—

DR. CHAPMAN: No. No, thank you. I prefer sugar. Particularly with chocolate chip cookies. (*As he takes a bite.*) They're delicious. You made them?

THOMAS (*as he sits*): Yes. I must confess.
For a beat, they all nibble cookies, sip tea.

THOMAS: Well. (*He takes a breath.*) Would you care for a little—(*Smiling, shrugging at his own nervousness, he tries for a little joke.*) I don't know what. I've offered all that we have.
He's interrupted as ANTHONY *returns his partly eaten cookie to the table.*

THOMAS: Don't you like it?

ANTHONY: No, no, it's delicious.

THOMAS: Then eat it, please.

ANTHONY: It's the diarrhea, Thomas. I'm afraid to have too much. I—but it tasted delicious. You go ahead.

DR. CHAPMAN: Your diarrhea is bad?

ANTHONY: Savage.

THOMAS: He suffers terribly.

DR. CHAPMAN: Is there no relief? Have you tried—

ANTHONY: We've tried everything.

THOMAS: It only seems to get worse.

ANTHONY: I'm tired. Always. And it has no pleasure in it, this tiredness, like the exhaustion from a game, or work. The exhaustion of life has a certain pleasure. You feel a kind of vitality rekindling itself. This is something else deep inside me. It empties me, this weariness. There's no rest for it. It leaves me depressed when I was never depressed in my life. Never. And this. (*He points to a place between his nose and his eye.*) Yesterday, this showed up. Popping out of me.

DR. CHAPMAN (*leaning in, examining*): I noticed.

ANTHONY: He noticed, Thomas. And you told me they were less conspicuous. Kaposi's sarcoma and its tasteless little parade of fucking tumors.
    THOMAS *points to* ANTHONY's *cheek, where a sore seeps out from the beard.*

THOMAS: There's another.

ANTHONY: A new one?

THOMAS: I think so. Is that one, Dr. Chapman?

DR. CHAPMAN: Yes.

ANTHONY: The beard cannot hide them all. (*Suddenly, he groans and clutches his abdomen.*) Ohhh, Thomas, I must go to the bath—help me, quickly. (*He tries to get up, then sags back.*) Ohhhhh. Dammit. Dammit. I'm sorry. I'm sorry. I have gone in my pants. Such a foul odor. Instantly. Rot. I am rot inside. The hemorrhoids burn. I must go change. (*He looks at* DR. CHAPMAN *coldly.*) I want to die.

DR. CHAPMAN: Is it so bad?

ANTHONY: Do you have to ask? (*Whirling to* THOMAS.) He asks! (*Then back to* DR. CHAPMAN.) Yes. (*And again to* THOMAS.) Take me to the bedroom to change. I want him to see me naked. Then he will know. Will you come with us, Dr. Chapman?

DR. CHAPMAN: Today you want to die, but in a few days, or a few hours even, you may—

ANTHONY: Wait and look. Then talk to me about tomorrow. (*He tries to get to his feet.*)

THOMAS (*helping*): He's very upset.

ANTHONY: Of course I'm upset. Just help me, just help me. No, no, wait. (*He sags back onto the couch.*) I'm woozy.

"Woozy." What a word. Woozy. Woozy. Woozy. I am woozy and I may puke. But I want you to see. In a minute.

DR. CHAPMAN: All right.

ANTHONY: I wear a diaper. I want you to see—I wear a diaper. It is humiliating. But I want you to see. I am sores. I am nothing. You must see. Sores and shit. And blood.

DR. CHAPMAN: Are there no good days? You have no relief?

ANTHONY: Sleep. When I sleep. The hours of sleep are good, and so I think of dying. It's the forgetfulness that makes me want to—that teaches me to die. I am not a man who would have ever thought of such a thing—to take my life. Never before this. Never! My life was my treasure. But it's gone. Taken from me.

THOMAS: I have to wash you—I have to clean you.

ANTHONY: Yes.

THOMAS: Come. Now. Can we go now.

ANTHONY: All right. (*He rises, with* THOMAS's *help.*)

THOMAS: Come along.
They make their way upstage, passing DR. CHAPMAN.

ANTHONY: Two woozy friends. (ANTHONY *falters.*) Owww, owww, owww.

THOMAS: I'm sorry, I'm sorry.

ANTHONY: I know, I know. Owww, owww. Ohhhhhhhh.

THOMAS: I'm so sorry.
At the edge of the stage, THOMAS *and* ANTHONY *stop in shadows, leaning against each other.* DR. CHAPMAN *faces out in a narrowing pool of light.*

DR. CHAPMAN: I followed them into their bedroom where Anthony lay on his side on the bed, offering his lesions to me as evidence. I stared. His anus was a large circular ulceration, oozing blood. His buttocks were smeared with pus and liquid stool. Tenderly, Thomas bathed him and dressed him in a fresh diaper, and I watched. Even though I had been summoned there, I felt a kind of voyeur. I felt rude and unnecessary and indecent.
As the lights come back up, THOMAS *and* ANTHONY *separate and look downstage at* DR. CHAPMAN.

THOMAS: He knows now, Anthony.

ANTHONY: Does he?

DR. CHAPMAN: Yes. Are there no good days?

ANTHONY: This is a good day. Because you are here this is a wonderful day. A . . . *(He curses exuberantly in Spanish.)* . . . day!
DR. CHAPMAN *stares at* ANTHONY, *who moves to settle onto the couch.*

THOMAS: Would you like another cup of tea, Dr. Chapman?

DR. CHAPMAN: No.

THOMAS: I could make some coffee.

DR. CHAPMAN: No.
> As DR. CHAPMAN *settles in the chair adjacent to the* *couch,* ANTHONY *motions for* THOMAS *to join him on the* *couch.*

THOMAS (*settling on the couch*): Another cookie?

DR. CHAPMAN: No.

ANTHONY: A friend in Colombia, a doctor friend, is mailing what I have been told is to be a lethal dose of barbiturates. They will arrive soon.

DR. CHAPMAN: I see.

ANTHONY: But what I fear is that something could go wrong and I would—I would—

THOMAS: It might not work.

ANTHONY: Dr. Nagle at the clinic refuses to advise me—he won't even talk to me about it.

THOMAS: There are so many patients.

ANTHONY: When all I want is to be able to be certain somehow that it not fail.

THOMAS: He worries that he won't do it right.

DR. CHAPMAN: It's actually quite difficult to do correctly.

THOMAS: But what could be so hard? Don't you just take them?

ANTHONY: That's what I'm frightened of. It has to be . . . difficult. That's why I desire assistance. Someone to help me, Dr. Chapman.

DR. CHAPMAN: I know that's what you think you want, Anthony.

ANTHONY: But if someone was with me to inject an additional dose into me . . . a fatal dose . . . if the pills failed.

DR. CHAPMAN: I can't do that. That's not why I'm here, Anthony. I'm here to discuss certain things—I mean, perhaps I could teach you the proper way to take the pills.

ANTHONY: Yes. Yes.

THOMAS: But don't you just take them?

ANTHONY: I've been trying to tell you, Thomas—the body fights, the body is a deceiver. That's why I must have help—and I must do it soon, while I have the strength and courage, and I must have Thomas with me. That's why he must be there, holding me. So I have the courage. We have discussed these matters, and he wants to be with me. Would you approve of that, Dr. Chapman? That I have company? (*Turning to* THOMAS.) And he must not cry. You must promise not to cry.

THOMAS: But that's not fair. It's not fair to ask me not to cry.

ANTHONY: I couldn't bear it if you cried.

THOMAS: What if I just—if it just happens?

ANTHONY: I make this request to you. You must discipline yourself.

THOMAS: He can't make me promise that, can he, Dr. Chapman?

DR. CHAPMAN: I don't think, Anthony, that a person's emotions can be promised in such circumstances. You can ask him to be with you, and to do his best not to cry, but more than that—well, it's the kind of thing, Anthony, that if he did promise, he would be lying. You can ask him to promise that he will try. He can promise to try, but—

ANTHONY: Will you promise to try?

THOMAS: I won't be able to do it.

ANTHONY: But will you try?

THOMAS (*leaping up, turning away, enraged*): It's so awful. The whole thing. I hate the whole thing; it makes me furious. Honest to God.
Beeping offstage.

ANTHONY: My pill.
THOMAS *hurries off the upstage right corner.*

THOMAS: Yes. Yes.

DR. CHAPMAN: What is it you're taking?

ANTHONY: I take everything, Doctor. This one is for pain. But I have chests and dressers full of pills. Jewel cases. They are my jewels.

THOMAS (*as he returns with a pill and a glass of water*): We've tried everything—every experimental drug and protocol for the diarrhea, but nothing works.

ANTHONY: And the chemotherapy seems to assist the tumors. They flourish in it. My mouth is covered with them. Look.
ANTHONY *opens his mouth, and* DR. CHAPMAN *looks inside.*

THOMAS: I think they were actually quite a bit worse several days ago. I know you've nothing to compare them to, but they have in fact to some degree—diminished.

ANTHONY (*reaching to take* THOMAS's *hand*): Thomas believes in God, don't you, Thomas. (*Kissing the hand.*) He prays.

DR. CHAPMAN: Do you pray, Anthony?

ANTHONY: Nothing can happen to me now, Dr. Chapman, except my death. It is the only act of significance left for me that I can dictate, that I can choose. To pick the time and method. To defy this monster. To say, I, Anthony, live. And now I do this thing that you, Death, have so far failed to do. I will do it! At this moment, Dr. Chapman, I am still able. But soon it will be beyond me. Then I will be the victim in every way.

DR. CHAPMAN: But you see, the thing is that it's not—how can I say this? Death—actual death is not something—you see, what you do, what you're thinking, is you take the pills—and that is what you do—you're right. You take the pills. But that's not death. You can't do it. It's never ours to govern. You do something—but you do not do IT. You take pills, and death occurs. But—

ANTHONY (*leaning in*): You're going to do it, aren't you. You're going to help me.
DR. CHAPMAN *rises, pacing away from them.*

DR. CHAPMAN: The barbiturates coming from Colombia are what kind?

ANTHONY: Bellergals. A hundred milligrams. I have been guaranteed at least a hundred pills. They will arrive soon. (*Moving after* DR. CHAPMAN.) Tell me you're going to do it, Dr. Chapman.

DR. CHAPMAN: Have you discussed this with anyone else? I mean, these ideas?

THOMAS: Why?

ANTHONY: Well, of course with some—a few people.

DR. CHAPMAN: I think it would be wise to limit the number—the people who might know. To keep it confined.

THOMAS: Are you worried about the police?

ANTHONY: We've only told a few people.

DR. CHAPMAN: Tell no one else.

THOMAS: No.

ANTHONY: We won't.

THOMAS: We could go to jail, couldn't we. If—I mean, if we actually—if you—

DR. CHAPMAN: I think we should be very careful. There are those who would rush to punish us.

THOMAS: I've never done anything like this. I've never broken the law. Because that's what we'll be doing. We'll be breaking the law. And, I mean, we could be caught. We'd be accomplices or something then, Dr. Chapman—is that right?

ANTHONY: I don't think Dr. Chapman is worried about that.

THOMAS: Of course he is, and I am too. Because I'm the sole beneficiary in Anthony's will. Do you see what I mean, Dr. Chapman?

DR. CHAPMAN: Is that right, Anthony?

THOMAS: If I receive everything he has, and there's any suspicion, wouldn't that—?

ANTHONY: I want you to have my possessions.

THOMAS: I know, but it could look as if—

ANTHONY: I want to talk about this later, Thomas. This is not pertinent to the things I need to straighten out with Dr.—

THOMAS: I know that. But I'm not talking about you at this particular instant. You won't be a part of this if we're caught, because you won't be here anymore. You'll be—

ANTHONY: Dead.

THOMAS: He just doesn't have any idea how this is for me. Because it's worse for him, I know it is—but it's SOMETHING for me. And he acts sometimes like it's NOTHING—like I don't have my own feelings about all this.

So he wants me with him when it happens, and I want that too—I want to be with him. But I've never seen anyone die.

DR. CHAPMAN: Of course.

THOMAS: And he forbids me to cry. I can't be there feeling that I'm doing something wrong, that I'm ruining everything if I have emotions that I can't control.

DR. CHAPMAN: Of course not. You see that, Anthony, don't you?

THOMAS: I mean, if I'm there, and I'm holding you and you die—do you understand what I mean?

ANTHONY: You're right, Thomas—I'm sorry, I lose track. I'm sorry. I'm self-absorbed.
As ANTHONY *moves back,* THOMAS *eases to him and touches him, embraces him.*

THOMAS: And why wouldn't you be? He suffers so. How could he not be? I understand that. But still—still—there are other things.

ANTHONY: You're right, Thomas. You're right. I'm sorry.

THOMAS: You don't have to be sorry. Why should you be sorry?
As they embrace, DR. CHAPMAN *turns and strides upstage toward his coat, which is draped over a chair.* THOMAS *looks, then sees where* DR. CHAPMAN *is going.*

THOMAS: Are you going?

DR. CHAPMAN: Yes, I think . . .

THOMAS: Let me help you with your coat.
ANTHONY coughs as THOMAS hurries to retrieve the coat and DR. CHAPMAN moves to ANTHONY.

DR. CHAPMAN: All those people that you've told what you're contemplating—try not to talk to them anymore.

ANTHONY: Yes.

DR. CHAPMAN: And, I'm thinking, Anthony, do you have a good lawyer?

ANTHONY: Yes. Very much so.

DR. CHAPMAN: Because you should arrange a codicil to your will requesting that there be no autopsy.

ANTHONY: I knew you'd decide to help me. I was right, wasn't I.

DR. CHAPMAN: I will help you, Anthony. But not to the extent you want.

ANTHONY: Please.

THOMAS: You mustn't count on that, Anthony. You'll only be disappointed.
ANTHONY reaches and takes DR. CHAPMAN's hand.

ANTHONY: Dr. Chapman. You asked, Do I pray? Now I pray to you. Don't be troubled. You will be the instrument that I will use. That's all. Think of it that way. You are an instrument. No more; no less. I will use you. For my rescue. *(He kisses DR. CHAPMAN's hand; he kisses the buttons on DR. CHAPMAN's coat sleeve.)* For my rescue.
THOMAS *stands watching, as* DR. CHAPMAN *and* ANTHONY

study each other, and the emotion between them. DR.
CHAPMAN *steps away, heads for the door.*

DR. CHAPMAN: Good night.

THOMAS: Good night.

ANTHONY: Thank you, Dr. Chapman.
The lights dim on ANTHONY *and* THOMAS, *as* DR. CHAPMAN,
*alone now on the upstage left corner of the ramp, faces
out. Music plays in the background.*

DR. CHAPMAN: An instrument. He wants me to become his
instrument. (*Walking downstage.*) Anthony's instrument. Then I would be—what would I be? A means for
him—this other person—this Anthony to enact his will?
(*Crossing the front of the stage, he moves to his chair and
phone.*) Like a forceps or a scalpel when I held them. He
wants me to be that simple. As for my own feelings?
Ignore them. Regarding my reservations—that uneasy
murmuring just beyond the horizon of my thoughts—
ignore that too. Governed only by his aims, I would be like
the scalpel, innocent and free of being what I am, a man.
*A loud blast of amplified sound: a radio sportscaster cov-
ering hockey. The lights take* DR. CHAPMAN *into dark.
The slide comes on: JANUARY 24, 1990.*
    On the stage left corner, the DOORMAN *is sweeping
with a large push broom across the front of the stage.*

VOICE OF SPORTSCASTER: Skating four on four. Leetch feeds the
puck to Turcotte. He's got it. Slides it to Gartner.

DOORMAN: Attaboy, Garty. You're the boss, Garty, show them
why!

VOICE OF SPORTSCASTER: He's looking. He's waiting. Back to Turcotte. He's looking. Fires a shot, off the stick. Rebound. Shot by Gartner.

DOORMAN (*stops sweeping, struggling to help the team*): C'mon, c'mon!

VOICE OF SPORTSCASTER: Stick save. Long rebound to the wing! Leetch is there. He sends a blast. It's off the post.

DOORMAN: Damn!
DR. CHAPMAN *walks past the* DOORMAN, *who looks up.*

DOORMAN: Hey, Doc. Leetch just missed off the post.

DR. CHAPMAN (*seeing* Eddie): Oh. Eddie. Hello.

DOORMAN: Can you believe it?

DR. CHAPMAN: Who missed?

DOORMAN: Leetch! Can you believe it?

DR. CHAPMAN: Oh. Too bad.
DR. CHAPMAN *moves on along the ramp, heading upstage to the stage left corner, with the* DOORMAN *trailing along behind him, sweeping.*

DOORMAN: Too bad? Doc, no, no, "too bad" doesn't cover it. This isn't too bad. This is a catastrophe. It's a hex. The franchise is hexed. I'm hexed.
As a doorbell rings loudly, the DOORMAN *wheels offstage, and* DR. CHAPMAN *steps up onto the raked platform where* ANTHONY *waits near the couch.*

ANTHONY: *Buenos días,* Dr. Chapman.

DR. CHAPMAN: Hello, Anthony.
    ANTHONY *steps toward* DR. CHAPMAN *and takes* DR.
    CHAPMAN'S *coat.* ANTHONY *is in pain, which he makes little
    effort to conceal. He drops the coat, and* DR. CHAPMAN
    bends to pick it up.

DR. CHAPMAN: There, there. I'll get that.

ANTHONY: No, no.
    They are almost struggling over the fallen coat, as THOMAS
    *comes out of the bedroom, buttoning his jacket. He races
    toward them.*

THOMAS: I'm sorry, I haven't left yet—I know you said you
    needed to see Anthony alone, but I—anyway, I'll be out
    of here in a moment.

DR. CHAPMAN: I thought some things might be simpler if
    Anthony and I could—

THOMAS: Fine, fine. Whatever.

DR. CHAPMAN: It has to do with my sense of the doctor–
    patient relationship, I suppose—that—

THOMAS: You don't have to explain. Just tell me how long I
    should stay away.

DR. CHAPMAN: An hour should be sufficient.

THOMAS: Then I'll just stay out for two hours. In order to make
    certain I don't intrude. Good-bye.

He shakes hands with DR. CHAPMAN *and then gives* ANTHONY *a peck on the cheek.*

THOMAS: Bye-bye, Anthony.

DR. CHAPMAN: Good-bye.

ANTHONY: Bye-bye.
  As he goes out the door, DR. CHAPMAN *and* ANTHONY *face each other.*

ANTHONY: I have the barbiturates. (*He pulls the vial from his robe.*) They arrived from Colombia.

DR. CHAPMAN: Let me take a look.
  DR. CHAPMAN *takes the pills, studying the vial.*

ANTHONY: I hope there's enough. I have new lesions every day.
  ANTHONY *pulls up his shirt.* DR. CHAPMAN *looks at the sores, his fingers hesitant to touch the wounds.*

ANTHONY: They sprout from me. It is my anger I think that fertilizes them.

DR. CHAPMAN: How are your other symptoms?

ANTHONY: The diarrhea is unrelenting. Are there enough pills?

DR. CHAPMAN: Oh, yes. Three-quarters of this bottle, I would think, would deliver a lethal dosage.

ANTHONY: And do I just take them?

DR. CHAPMAN: No, no.

ANTHONY (*miming dumping the pills into his mouth*): I mean, get them into me quick and fast!

DR. CHAPMAN: No, no, no. That's what you can't do—just throw them down. This is the issue we had under discussion the other day, if you recall. At least I alluded to it. Let me get some water, and I'll try and point out the pitfalls. (*He starts for the kitchen, then steps back.*) It must be done very carefully. Very consciously. (*Heading off to the kitchen.*) You must be disciplined. We can't predict your emotions at that moment. (*Talking from off, now.*) Certainly I can't say, and I doubt that even you can anticipate your own state of mind at that moment— when the time actually comes—the turmoil. (*Returning.*) Or perhaps calm. And your physical condition will be changing as the time passes. That has to be taken into account. Which is why you have to know exactly what to do.

ANTHONY *settles on the chair adjacent to the couch, and* DR. CHAPMAN *settles onto the couch. He holds a glass of water and takes a bottle of aspirin from his pocket.*

DR. CHAPMAN: I have some baby aspirin here that I'll use to show you. And this water.

ANTHONY: I will be your perfect student in this matter, Dr. Chapman.

DR. CHAPMAN *scatters a few aspirins on the table.*

DR. CHAPMAN: What you must above all do is take little sips and only one pill at a time, or else you will vomit them up. Let me show you. (*He carefully places one pill on his tongue, then takes an exaggeratedly tiny little bitty sip of water.*) You see? Tiny sips.

Anthony: Let me try.
*Anthony reaches for the glass and one of the spilled pills.
Dr Chapman watches closely as Anthony takes a pill.*

Dr. Chapman: Tiny tiny sips. As little water as possible.
As Anthony prepares to take a second aspirin:

Dr. Chapman: Even less water, Anthony. You must not take them too fast or with too much water. That's what you have to understand. And yet, you must not go too slowly. That's the paradox. Because if you go too slowly, if you take too much time, the drug begins to affect you and slow you before you're finished and then you simply go to sleep without having taken in enough for the cumulative effect to be deadly.

Anthony: And then I would just wake up? Just sleep and wake up?

Dr. Chapman: I'm afraid so.

Anthony: Be rigorous in your instruction, Dr. Chapman.

Dr. Chapman: Less water. Do it again.
As Anthony tries with another aspirin:

Dr. Chapman: Rigorous is what you must be, Anthony. Stern with yourself on that night. This is what's crucial. Little sips at a regular pace.

Anthony: Is this good—this pace?

Dr. Chapman: I think so. Methodical. Establish a count. Like one, two, three, pill. One, two, three, pill.

ANTHONY: One, two, three—(*He pops a pill into his mouth and drinks, then suddenly starts to cough and choke.*)

DR. CHAPMAN (*leaning in, helping, offering a handkerchief*): You must not fill up and vomit. And yet you must not go so slowly that you run the risk of—well—

ANTHONY: Getting "woozy." And we don't want that, do we? We don't want Anthony getting "woozy."

DR. CHAPMAN: No, we don't.

ANTHONY: Too "woozy" to kill himself. (*Suddenly facing* DR. CHAPMAN, *imploring him.*) Couldn't you be there with me so you could inject more of the drug if necessary? If I failed, if I fell asleep? (*Rising, he rolls up his sleeve, showing his forearm.*) I have good veins. Do you see? There are several needle marks, puncture marks—where blood has been drawn. Who would ever notice one more mark in the midst of this mess? It would have to go undetected, wouldn't it? You would be there then. And if you were there, I would have the courage.

DR. CHAPMAN: Do you have any family in this country?

ANTHONY: Why? Oh, no, no. They're all in Colombia—in Medellín. Four sisters, three brothers. They all live in Medellín.

DR. CHAPMAN: What have you told them?

ANTHONY: Of this? Ohh, nothing. No, no. (*He turns away, a little agitated.*)

DR. CHAPMAN: You must. You must tell them.

ANTHONY: It isn't possible, Dr. Chapman.

DR. CHAPMAN: Anthony, I must advise you in the strongest
terms—you must speak to them.

ANTHONY: They know nothing about my life, my situation—
they—

DR. CHAPMAN: None of them?

ANTHONY: One brother, but—well—my mother, you see, she
has no formal education, though she is very wise. I think
of her as one of the truly wise. And yet we have failed
somehow to discuss my life. She knows neither that I
am gay nor that I am ill.

DR. CHAPMAN: But that's all the more reason for you to tell
her now. Think through the implications of not telling
her. She will conclude that you have committed suicide
for some ordinary, petty reason.

ANTHONY: I have written her a letter that will be sent after my
death. It will tell of my love for her, and it will thank
her for all she has done. But nothing more.

DR. CHAPMAN: I find this very disturbing, Anthony. I hate to
contest a point of such an obviously personal nature, but—

ANTHONY: It will be enough. My older brother, Esteban, he is
the one who knows that I am gay, and for him it is a
disgrace. My death will relieve him. It will verify his
point of view. He has forbidden me to tell the others in
my family. Esteban, my sisters—and all my brothers,
too—they are all living around my mother. There are
twelve grandchildren. She will not be alone.

ANTHONY *smiles, then looks weary and gestures to the couch on which* DR. CHAPMAN *sits.*

ANTHONY: I must lie down.

DR. CHAPMAN (*leaping up guiltily*): Of course. I'm sorry. Perhaps I've pushed too hard.

ANTHONY: No, no. (*He sags onto the couch and lies there.*) I just need a moment. There's wine if you would care for some.

DR. CHAPMAN: No, no. (*He stands over Anthony, looking down at him.*)

ANTHONY: It's in the refrigerator. (*Playful.*) And there's still some cookies. In the canister by the stove.

DR. CHAPMAN (*thinking hard*): Well . . . maybe. (*He heads off.*)

ANTHONY: Yes, why don't you. . . . I have always counted so much on my spirit. My vigor. I had great energy all my life—a vitality that I could count on. Along with my looks. My looks were my way through the world. I had . . . charm. . . .
As DR. CHAPMAN *returns with a cookie and a glass of milk,* ANTHONY *sits up on the couch.*

ANTHONY: Did you find everything?

DR. CHAPMAN: Yes. (*He settles down on the chair next to the couch; he nibbles his cookie, sips his milk.*)

ANTHONY: No, no, no, in Colombia one is better off not to be a homosexual, or at least not to know it if they are. Until

I was eight years old or so, I was in such useful ignorance,
but then it all changed.

DR. CHAPMAN: You changed at eight?

ANTHONY: Oh, yes. These feelings piercing my childhood, this
undeniable attraction to men. It was not so much my self
changing, it was more exactly my understanding that
changed. A strange blooming in a field of perfect ignorance. I struggled, of course, with the common confu-
sions. Though they scarcely mattered, because it was
impossible to express them, these feelings, even if I had
understood them fully. Even much later, at the university in Bogotá where I went to study, and where I lived
for six years, in an apartment with six other male stu-
dents, I did not express it. It was a quiet student life. We
were friends, that's all. Then I came to New York, lived
in freedom.

DR. CHAPMAN: I guess that was a relief for you.

ANTHONY: It was fun. I was a wild boy on the loose at a carnival—I was wild . . . and foolish, too, I guess. (*Sitting up.*)
Were you ever a wild boy at the carnival, Dr. Chapman?

DR. CHAPMAN: What? Me? No. (*Laughs.*) Goodness.

ANTHONY: Chasing nurses.

DR. CHAPMAN: You mean around the desk? Like in a cartoon?

ANTHONY: Yes.

DR. CHAPMAN: No. (*Laughing softly.*) Well . . . (*Thinking.*) . . .
once.

ANTHONY: I knew it.

DR. CHAPMAN: When—when did you meet Thomas?

ANTHONY: I traveled here to attend NYU. That's when I met him and fell in love with him. This was in 1980. When my studies were complete we separated for two years, as people do when they misunderstand the deepest design of their lives. But we had the wisdom to stay in contact. Those two years ended, as if they had been imposed and we began to live together. When I fell ill, it was just an infection, I was certain, though I worried about AIDS. I told Thomas at once, and we agreed that we must discontinue sex and so we did. From that day forward, aside from mutual caressing, there has been no sexual contact between us. And this has had its difficulties of course, but they have been of surprisingly little consequence, because, as it turns out, it was not sex that mattered so much between us ever anyway—not really—it was not sex that kept us together, or brought us together in the first place. It was love. Always love.

DR. CHAPMAN: I see.

ANTHONY: Does this embarrass you?

DR. CHAPMAN: What?

ANTHONY: This intimacy. This . . . confession.

DR. CHAPMAN: No.

ANTHONY: I think it does. What is your first name, Dr. Chapman?

DR. CHAPMAN: Robert.

ANTHONY: I thought it was what you wanted, Robert, and so I talked, I mean, of my life; and I wanted that too, a chance for us to know one another better, to know one another in some way, if we are to share the moment—that moment of my death. (*Slight pause.*) I was right?

DR. CHAPMAN: When would you want this to happen?

ANTHONY: It must be soon. Soon. (*Getting to his feet.*) Let me— come with me. There's a calendar here.
He walks upstage to a table. He picks up a desk calendar and studies it.

ANTHONY: We're in January, so we need some time . . . all of us . . . to prepare. But I don't dare delay too long or . . . (*Studying the calendar.*) Are you free on February tenth?
DR. CHAPMAN *takes his pocket calendar out and turns some pages.*

ANTHONY: It's a Saturday. Saturday the tenth of February. It's far enough away to allow for the necessary. . . . Well, how does it look to you?

DR. CHAPMAN: The tenth. Yes. I'm free. I have one thing, but I'm sure I can switch it.

ANTHONY: February tenth. It seems all right?

DR. CHAPMAN: Yes. I think so.

ANTHONY: Shall we wait until you're certain you can change what you have, or—

DR. CHAPMAN: No, no, I can get rid of that.

ANTHONY: So we have a date?

DR. CHAPMAN: We have a date.
They close the books.

ANTHONY: You should talk now. You should tell me of yourself. So I know who it is I am to die with.

DR. CHAPMAN: I have not agreed to be with you, Anthony. I have not agreed to administer a shot. Have you misunderstood?

ANTHONY: Then why did we pick the day? A day that would be good for both of us?

DR. CHAPMAN (*moving away*): We were just picking the day. So you would know. So you could prepare.

ANTHONY (*following*): I see. Well, I would still like to know more of you. Are you native in New York?

DR. CHAPMAN: There's nothing very much to tell. Really. Besides, Thomas will be along in a moment.

ANTHONY: Now, I know that is a lie. I know there is so much to tell.

DR. CHAPMAN: No, no, not really.

ANTHONY: Please. About the nurse you chased.
Suddenly there is the noise of a door off left, and they look.

THOMAS (*calling from off*): Hello—I'm back.

DR. CHAPMAN: Hello, Thomas.
THOMAS strides on, removing his scarf, unbuttoning his jacket.

THOMAS: Hello, Dr. Chapman. Hello, An-thony.

ANTHONY: We have decided.

THOMAS: What?

ANTHONY: We have decided, Thomas. Dr. Chapman helped me.

THOMAS: Decided what? What's he saying, Dr. Chapman?

DR. CHAPMAN: We picked the day. He did, really. February tenth.

THOMAS: You decided? Are you saying—? Are you saying that . . . ?

ANTHONY: Yes.

THOMAS: When? When did you decide?

ANTHONY: Just now.
The lights go to black and then rise on THOMAS alone near the upstage left corner, a telephone held to his ear. Music plays in the background.

THOMAS *(into phone)*: Susanah? Susanah, they've decided. They're going through with it. . . . No, no, they picked a date, he and this doctor I told you about. I wasn't even there. I was out—just out. Can I ask you something? I came back and they told me. Can I ask you something? I feel so lost. I want you to help me get through this. I need you to help us both get through this.

A loud blast of sound: amplified voice of a sportscaster.
Hockey game in progress. On the screen is projected:
JANUARY 29, 1990.

   The lights come up on the downstage left corner where
the DOORMAN *and* DR. CHAPMAN *stand side by side, gaz-*
ing upward, almost reverential as they listen to the
game.

VOICE OF SPORTSCASTER: Hunter powers over the blue line, dinks, fakes a shot, fakes a shot. Then . . . SHOOTS! Save by Richter. Point-blank save by Richter. Shot by Muriev. Save by Richter. Rebound. SAVE BY RICHTER! SAVE BY RICHTER! SAVE BY RICHTER! ANOTHER SAVE BY RICHTER!

DOORMAN: What a stand by Richter! Six—Five—no, six saves by Richter. You a hockey fan, Doc?

DR. CHAPMAN: Well, no.

DOORMAN: Oh, you oughta give it a try.

DR. CHAPMAN: I'm afraid I don't know anything about it, really.

DOORMAN: It's a great game! Would you go with me, if I got tickets sometime? As my guest. It'd be my honor, Doc.

DR. CHAPMAN: Well, I'm—I don't know.

DOORMAN: It's not what you think. No, no, the violence is not the game. The game is speed and instinct. They're like birds. It's an electric current.

DR. CHAPMAN: I don't think so, Eddie. Thank you, but—

DOORMAN: Just tell me this, tell me one thing. What could you lose by going to one game?

DR. CHAPMAN: I don't know.

DOORMAN: Well, I do. I know. And I can tell you, too. Nothing. I'm gonna call this guy right now and fix it! (*Heading off, grabbing phone.*) We're gonna have two tickets in the front row, Doc! You'll love it!
   As the DOORMAN disappears, the doorbell rings. SUSANAH TOMKINS enters from stage right on the platform. DR. CHAPMAN turns and finds himself face-to-face with her.

SUSANAH: Hello.

DR. CHAPMAN: Oh, am I—where am I? Is this the right apartment? What apartment is this?

THOMAS (*as he comes running forward, entering from upstage right*): Dr. Chapman, this is Susanah Tomkins.

DR. CHAPMAN: Oh. Hello.

SUSANAH: We've met. (*She extends her hand.*)

DR. CHAPMAN: We have?

SUSANAH: Yes.
   As they shake hands:

SUSANAH: At the Levines'.

DR. CHAPMAN: Oh. Yes.

SUSANAH: You don't remember.
    ANTHONY *enters, wearing a bright red silk shirt.*

ANTHONY: Dr. Chapman. Good evening.

THOMAS: Chiquito! You're wearing your new shirt!

DR. CHAPMAN: Thomas, can I talk to you for a second?

THOMAS: Of course.

DR. CHAPMAN (*heading for the upstage right corner, near the kitchen*): We'll just be a minute.

THOMAS (*moving to join* DR. CHAPMAN): I've put some water on for tea.
    As SUSANAH *joins* ANTHONY *on the couch:*

ANTHONY: Is something wrong?

SUSANAH: I don't think it's serious.
    Up in the corner, in a pocket of light, DR. CHAPMAN, *clearly disturbed, faces* THOMAS.

DR. CHAPMAN: What is she doing here?

THOMAS: Well, she's a friend. No, no, you don't have to worry—she's fine.

DR. CHAPMAN: What do you mean, "she's fine"?

THOMAS: She's all right. She knows everything.

DR. CHAPMAN: What are you talking about? We—we agreed to keep this between ourselves, between the three of us.

THOMAS: But she can be trusted completely. She's my dearest friend. She's our friend, Anthony's friend, my friend.

DR. CHAPMAN: That's not what I'm saying. I'm saying that you and I and Anthony agreed to restrict, to confine—we were going to limit the people who—

SUSANAH: Is this about me?

DR. CHAPMAN: It's not so much about you . . .
As SUSANAH *strides up to them:*

DR. CHAPMAN: . . . as it is about certain agreements that I thought Thomas and I had reached that were unequivocal.

SUSANAH: There's nothing to worry about. I understand the delicacy of the situation. Of course you're nervous about me just appearing like this—

THOMAS: I should have told you, I know—warned you, but—

SUSANAH: He should have.

THOMAS: I'm sorry.

DR. CHAPMAN: I don't understand how you could violate our ground rules without giving me the slightest warning.

SUSANAH: That's why I'm here, really. I mean, to tell you.

THOMAS: To ask you, in a sense.

DR. CHAPMAN: Ask me what?

THOMAS: I worried you would refuse me if I just asked. But if you met her—and saw how she—how WE—

SUSANAH: What you have to understand is the necessity—that I have to be involved. This is important . . . in my life. I can't tell you how important, but these two are the dearest people, my dearest friends. I can't be left out of this matter, this terrible—but I understand your shock.

THOMAS: It's perfectly understandable.

SUSANAH: I just want to reassure you. I understand the complexity, the delicacy, and how you would naturally be reluctant to have what appears to you as this total stranger brought in at this sensitive moment, but that's the point. I'm not a stranger.

THOMAS: She's been my confidante for years. And Anthony's, too.

SUSANAH: Do you understand? If it's come to this—that it's come to such a thing between these two, then I have to be with them. You've got to understand.

THOMAS: I need her to help me through this. To help us both.

SUSANAH: I'll make the tea. You go out there, the two of you. I'll join you. It'll be all right, Doctor. (*She steps offstage right.*)

ANTHONY (*calling to them*): What are the three of you concocting in there without me?

THOMAS: Nothing.

DR. CHAPMAN: Nothing.

ANTHONY: Someone come here. Anthony is alone.

THOMAS *hurries to* ANTHONY. SUSANAH, *carrying a tray with the tea, returns and faces* DR. CHAPMAN.

SUSANAH: You don't like me, do you?

DR. CHAPMAN: What?

SUSANAH: I can usually tell from the first instant.

DR. CHAPMAN: This isn't personal.

SUSANAH: Of course it is. But that's all right. I'm not here to challenge your authority.

DR. CHAPMAN: I don't know what you mean.

SUSANAH: Good. How do you like your tea?

DR. CHAPMAN: What do you mean?

SUSANAH: About the tea?

DR. CHAPMAN: No.

SUSANAH: Thomas called me—we met for a drink. He started sobbing. I'm here to help. That's all. We can't all be heroes, you know. As much as we'd like to be.

DR. CHAPMAN: Honestly, I'm having a certain amount of trouble understanding what you're really saying.

SUSANAH: Perhaps when you know me better.
As she strides down to the couch, the lights darken except for a pool around DR. CHAPMAN, *who faces out.*

Music plays in the background as he walks directly downstage.

DR. CHAPMAN: I was in surgery—this was a year and seven months ago. We were all scrubbed and masked. In our uniforms. The scalpel in my hand, and as I worked and my hand grew tired—it's difficult, you know. The flesh fights back. You have to force the blade. Force it. I went deeper, and then . . . I stopped. Everyone thought I was resting. They wiped my brow, and I stood there thinking that it was a person lying there and I was just this man with a knife. I finished, of course, and it was fine. Successful—as far as everyone else was concerned. But I thought I better take a little break. A day or two, a few weeks. I haven't picked up a scalpel since.
Behind him, the others laugh as they sit with their tea, and DR. CHAPMAN *moves to join them.*

SUSANAH: Well, I thought it was off the mark.

THOMAS: I have to admit that it is the kind of movie that invites you to be harsh in your criticism, but I still think a person can—

SUSANAH: I wasn't harsh on it. I took it on its own terms.

THOMAS: No, no, I mean, it has pretensions of being serious, but it's really intended purely as entertainment, and so if you are taken in by its less integral aspects, its more superficial kind of surface things, then you will misapply your own critical standards and judge it harshly. It's really slight, and if you look at it that way, it's quite fulfilling.

SUSANAH: I don't think it deserves that much thought, actually, for goodness' sake. I did nothing more than sit and react.

THOMAS: But what I'm doing is I'm just trying to hopefully kind of delineate where the sense of confusion in your response comes from, because I really think that's it.

SUSANAH: Maybe.

THOMAS: I'm sure of it.

ANTHONY: I didn't see it.

SUSANAH: You didn't miss much.

THOMAS: I liked it. I found it satisfying—but strictly on its own terms.

SUSANAH: Well, you could be right, I suppose, but I have no intention of testing your theory by seeing it again.

ANTHONY: You can rent the video in a few months.

SUSANAH: A dubious opportunity from where I'm sitting. A film like that is like Ben and Jerry's Marshmallow Dream for the mind. It's like injecting fat directly into your brain.

THOMAS: Please, Susanah, protect me from ever ending up on your worst-ten list.

SUSANAH: I am unforgiving, at least aesthetically.

ANTHONY: Robert.

DR. CHAPMAN: Yes.

ANTHONY: Tell me about death.

DR. CHAPMAN: What?

ANTHONY: What it's like, what happens.

DR. CHAPMAN: What do you mean?

ANTHONY: What happens when you die?

DR. CHAPMAN: Well—you mean you want me to tell you what happens when you die?

ANTHONY: You're a doctor; you should know.

DR. CHAPMAN: I don't know what you mean.

SUSANAH: Are you asking how does it manifest, Anthony? What does the body do?

ANTHONY: Yes.

SUSANAH: He's asking about the physical experience, Dr. Chapman, not—

DR. CHAPMAN: Oh! You mean in the body—is that what you mean?—the physical details! Anthony, I thought you—

ANTHONY: What? The afterlife? No, no, no.

SUSANAH: Why would he ask you about that?

ANTHONY (*little laugh*): No, no, I wouldn't ask that. In fact, I'll do my best to tell you about that when I get there. I'll report back.

DR. CHAPMAN: So it's the physical details you're inquiring about?

SUSANAH: Of course.

DR. CHAPMAN: Well. . . . Like what? Do you have some specific area that—

ANTHONY: The death rattle.

THOMAS: Is there such a thing?

DR. CHAPMAN: It's been called that.

SUSANAH: But that's not what it in fact is. I mean, "Death" rattling.

DR. CHAPMAN: Well, no. I mean, there's sometimes—actually, it's very common, that certain secretions in the lungs cannot be cleared, and the body—the body makes this last effort to clear them.

ANTHONY: The body is a single-minded bore. Live, live, live. That's all it wants. Is there anything I should have, something Thomas and I might not have thought of, so that I am prepared, so I am not caught off guard? Any kind of equipment we should buy to get ready?

DR. CHAPMAN: Not that I can think of at the moment. You have the diapers.

THOMAS: He has to die in diapers?

ANTHONY: Thomas, I think your fastidiousness makes you miss the point. I live in diapers.

THOMAS: I was thinking of your dignity.

ANTHONY: Ah. Yes. Well. Don't bother.

DR. CHAPMAN: You see there is at the time of death a relaxation of the bowel and the urinary sphincters, so that it would be best if—

THOMAS: I shouldn't have asked.

ANTHONY: You didn't. I'm the one that asked. I hadn't seen the movie. So I changed the subject. I'm the one that asked.

SUSANAH: That is what happened, Thomas.

THOMAS: And then I asked.

ANTHONY: No, you didn't.

THOMAS: Well I said something. And I shouldn't have. That's what I'm saying. (*Rising, starting to collect the teacups on the tray.*) Whatever I said when I thought I was asking was something I shouldn't have said. (*Moving upstage right with the loaded tray.*) We were having a nice conversation there and—I mean, it was almost as if we were just all together, having a nice evening, an ordinary, simple—(*He freezes, then turns to face them.*) I'm terrified of the police. I always have been. The idea, the idea— they terrify me. They can just take you and put you in jail. Put handcuffs on you. March you off and lock you up. Dr. Chapman, do you think that I should see a lawyer in order to prepare for what might happen? I mean, what if we're caught and I'm put—I'm put in prison? It could happen. It could. No one can tell me it couldn't. (*He begins to weep.*) And I'm losing Anthony. That's what I can't bear. Even as he is, with all his suffering, he's here. He's here! But if we do this he'll be gone and there's not a thing I can do about it.

THOMAS *turns and walks off.* ANTHONY *starts to rise and walk as* THOMAS *returns.* ANTHONY *moves to him.*

ANTHONY (*reaching to touch and console* THOMAS): Oh, please. Please, Thomas. It's all right.

THOMAS: It's not. It's not all right.

ANTHONY: Of course not, but—
DR. CHAPMAN *and* SUSANAH *watch as* THOMAS *and* ANTHONY *sag into each other's arms.*

SUSANAH (*spinning back, facing the table*): It's so fucking awful!

DR. CHAPMAN (*starting to rise*): I think—I don't think anybody's ready for this. Nobody's ready to do this. (*On his feet, he moves to his coat, which hangs over an upstage chair.*) Neither of you is ready, and to tell the truth, I'm not either.

THOMAS: What? No, no. What do you mean?

DR. CHAPMAN: It's obvious, isn't it? (*Heading for the door and looking back at her.*) Susanah?

SUSANAH: What?

ANTHONY (*pursuing* DR. CHAPMAN): No!

THOMAS: But Anthony, we have to listen to him if he thinks
we should put it off, or postpone it, or—

ANTHONY: Please. PLEASE! It's only a matter of a few minutes of misery for each of us, and then my misery will
be over—it will all be over. You will lose me anyway!
I'm gone anyway. I'm gone now!

THOMAS: Nooo, you're—

ANTHONY: This is not Anthony! This stinking baby in diapers
who cannot eat, who cannot think, is not a man! You
cannot be so selfish! You, Thomas; I need your commit-
ment most of all!

SUSANAH: But the certainty—the certainty is so difficult. I don't
know how anyone can know what is right absolutely in
this kind of situation.

ANTHONY: I do. I know.

DR. CHAPMAN: It's me. No, no, what I feel is that I'm putting
too much pressure on everything. (*Adjusting his coat.*)
My presence is demanding that you move from the level
of discussion, the level of possibility, into reality, into
action right now, when neither of you is—

ANTHONY: But that is why we wanted you here. It's why I
summoned you.
ANTHONY *pursues* DR. CHAPMAN, *and they pace along the
edge of the platform, moving downstage.*

DR. CHAPMAN: What I'm trying to say is that my involvement makes your death real, and near. It makes it close.

ANTHONY: I know.

DR. CHAPMAN: But Thomas—for Thomas, the whole matter is not as clear as it is for you.

ANTHONY: But I am the one who is to die.

DR. CHAPMAN: Yes, Anthony. You're resolved, but he isn't, and you demand his participation. I feel everything slipping because there are too many unsettled, unexamined feelings in this, so that it's slipping out of what little control I have—we have. I'm ready to withdraw. Now. I feel I should. I'm beginning to feel quite out of place.

ANTHONY: No. I beg you.

DR. CHAPMAN: Oppressive. I feel oppressive.

ANTHONY: Dr. Chapman—to move us to action is why we called you—

THOMAS: Dr. Chapman, please—this is my fault. (*Coming forward, interrupting.*) It's my fault. You're the answer to Anthony's prayers. To him you are a kind of salvation. (*He sits on the chair by the couch.*) You must not leave him. My feelings are not to be taken seriously—they must be seen as secondary, and they have to be subordinated by all of us to whatever Anthony wants.

DR. CHAPMAN: Susanah, what do you think?

SUSANAH: I feel I shouldn't intrude. I'm trying not to intrude.

DR. CHAPMAN: But what do you think? Honestly?

SUSANAH: It's your advice they want. It's you they're asking.
ANTHONY, *exhausted, moves toward the couch.*

ANTHONY: Thomas.

THOMAS: Yes.

ANTHONY: Thomas, listen. (*As he sags onto the couch and
faces* THOMAS.) I feel that perhaps I have asked too much
of you.

THOMAS: No. I will manage it.

ANTHONY: But if I didn't demand that you be with me, perhaps it would be easier.

THOMAS: What do you mean?

ANTHONY: Not with me when it happens.

THOMAS: Not with you? Not holding you? (*Moving to join*
ANTHONY *on the couch, taking his hand.*) You would be
alone.

ANTHONY: I would be with Dr. Chapman. It's too difficult for
you, Thomas. We both know it. You could be somewhere
else—with Susanah, perhaps.

THOMAS: No.

SUSANAH: You said your desires should be secondary, Thomas,
that you should subordinate yourself to what Anthony
wants. Did you really mean that?

THOMAS: Yes. I don't know. I'm saying a lot of things—

SUSANAH: I think you should listen to him.

ANTHONY (*to* DR. CHAPMAN): Thomas simply cannot lie. It's not in his nature. If he were questioned by the police, he would have to tell the truth. His attempts to lie would be hopeless. He simply can't. It's a virtue, really. (*To* THOMAS.) You know it's true, Thomas. (*To* DR. CHAPMAN.) We must find a way to help him be less involved. To protect him.

THOMAS: Where would I be, then? If I wasn't with you.

ANTHONY: I don't know.

SUSANAH: You could be with me. We could—

THOMAS: But Anthony, we've planned everything through so completely. I mean, the little things I was going to do for you. The lighting in the room, and the music that I would make sure was playing.

ANTHONY (*to* DR. CHAPMAN): We were going to play this Bach piece. To have it on the stereo as I took the pills.

THOMAS: You need that.

ANTHONY (*to* THOMAS): But *I* could do it. I could start the music. Make sure it started, and then I would take the pills as instructed by Robert. Who would maybe even be there with me to help me, to guide me. So I did it right.

THOMAS: And what would I do? Where would I be?

DR. CHAPMAN: You could wait in the living room with Susanah.

ANTHONY: You would not be with us.

SUSANAH: Does this make sense to you, Dr. Chapman? (*Approaching, she settles on the chair to the right of the couch.*) Does it seem feasible?

DR. CHAPMAN: I could be there. (*Approaching, he settles on the chair to the left of the couch.*) With him. To monitor him. And you and Thomas could—well, wait in the living room.

THOMAS: What are you saying? (*Rising, as if to escape their gathering.*) That we would be somewhere in the apartment waiting the whole time until he dies?

SUSANAH: We wouldn't have to. I mean, it wouldn't be necessary that we be here. We could go out—somewhere—and return to find him dead.

THOMAS: Where would we go?

SUSANAH: I don't know. Anywhere.

THOMAS (*pacing behind the couch*): It seems so weird when I think about it, just sitting in the living room, knowing what's going on in the next room.

SUSANAH: We could go out. I think we would have to. For a walk.

THOMAS: I couldn't just walk around.

SUSANAH: Or to the movies. We could go to the movies.

ANTHONY: What movie?

THOMAS: I don't know. Why?

ANTHONY: I was just wondering.

THOMAS: I don't know what movie. I don't know anything at this point.

SUSANAH: We would have to be out for how long? An hour? Two?

DR. CHAPMAN (*slipping out of his overcoat, leaving it on the chair on which he sits*): Oh, no. Much longer.

THOMAS: Longer? How long?

DR. CHAPMAN: Perhaps all day?

THOMAS: All day!
He approaches the others; they watch him.

THOMAS: I don't think I can stand it. This is insane. Listen to us. (*He stands looking down; these are the terms of his return.*) I don't think I can stand it. That's what I'm saying.

ANTHONY: It's all right.

THOMAS: Is it? IS IT? I have no idea. (*He sits again on the couch beside* ANTHONY.)

ANTHONY: But what will happen exactly?

SUSANAH: We'll come back. We'll find you.

THOMAS: And then what?

SUSANAH: We would have to call somebody, I would guess. A doctor.

DR. CHAPMAN: Yes. But not me.

THOMAS: Should it be the clinic? I'm not sure we should call the clinic.

DR. CHAPMAN: Well, somebody must be called.

SUSANAH: Nine-one-one?

THOMAS: What will they do? They'll be strangers, won't they?

DR. CHAPMAN: I think the clinic.

SUSANAH: All right then—and then what if they—what if the doctor notifies the police?

THOMAS: Yes, yes. Because Anthony makes no secret of his desires in this regard when he's at the clinic. Isn't that right, Anthony?

ANTHONY: Isn't what right?

THOMAS: That there are people at the clinic who know you want to die.

ANTHONY: I have spoken my heart, yes. Why?

THOMAS: They've even threatened to withhold pain medication because they thought him "high risk."

DR. CHAPMAN: Wait a minute! What have you told them, Anthony?

ANTHONY: I have never mentioned you, Dr. Chapman.

DR. CHAPMAN: This is very unnerving! (*Rising, he paces away.*) I mean, days ago, we spoke about this—we agreed that we required secrecy, that we required discretion, and then I come in here and find Susanah; now you're telling me that you go about just—when were you last at the clinic?

ANTHONY: It's not as if such sentiments are unique to me— don't think that.

DR. CHAPMAN: Well, what should I think?

ANTHONY: Such talk is quite common in our waiting room gatherings. Most express the desire to die at one point or another. Some die, others don't. It is not as if the things I've said set me apart in some particular, exaggerated way.

DR. CHAPMAN (*moving behind the couch, behind* ANTHONY): Anthony, listen to me. At the clinic, next time, I want you to do something for me.

ANTHONY: Yes, what?

DR. CHAPMAN: I want you to ask them for a prescription of fifty Levo-Dromoran tablets. It's a narcotic. They'll be useful to us. But, more importantly, it will give us a clear sense of how worried they are about you in this area. If they're really worried, they won't give them to you. Can you do that?

ANTHONY: All right. Yes, I'll ask them.

SUSANAH: You seem very disturbed on this point, Dr. Chapman.

DR. CHAPMAN: What we're talking about is against the law. We have to understand that no matter what our feelings of right or wrong, or compassion, or even moral authority, we are conspiring to commit an illegal, criminal act. And that is how we will be viewed if what we've done is discovered. We will be viewed as criminals. Murderers, even.

THOMAS: You're saying all this for my benefit, aren't you. Because of what I admitted about my feeling about jail. Just understand that I want to go forward. I'm sorry for my weakness in these things. We have to ignore it. I have to try to control it, but if I can't, then we must all ignore it. All of us.

SUSANAH: What are you thinking, Dr. Chapman?

DR. CHAPMAN (*grabbing his overcoat*): I'm quite late for another appointment. I really didn't expect things to get so complicated.

ANTHONY: You're going? But what is it? Can't you change it?

DR. CHAPMAN (*heading for the door*): No.

ANTHONY: I'll walk you to the door.

THOMAS: No, no. Let me; Anthony, you shouldn't—

ANTHONY: I want to. I can.
    As ANTHONY *follows* DR. CHAPMAN *toward the door:*

ANTHONY (*privately*): Where are you going?

DR. CHAPMAN: I told you. I have an appointment.

ANTHONY: Don't lie to me, Robert.

DR. CHAPMAN: I'm not—why would you say that?

ANTHONY: You're running away.

DR. CHAPMAN: No, no. I have an appointment. (*Calling.*) Good night, Thomas, Susanah.

THOMAS: Good night.

SUSANAH: Good night, Dr. Chapman. Thank you.
   DR. CHAPMAN *exits.*

THOMAS (*approaching* ANTHONY): You shouldn't exert yourself unnecessarily, like that. I could have walked him to the door.

ANTHONY: But I wanted to.

THOMAS: And so you did.

ANTHONY: That's right. I did. I'm worried he won't come back.

THOMAS: What did he say? Did he say that?

ANTHONY: No.
   ANTHONY *starts across from stage left to right.* THOMAS *reaches and touches* ANTHONY *as he passes.*

THOMAS: You think I'm driving him away, don't you.

ANTHONY: No.

THOMAS: You do.

ANTHONY: No. I'm going to bed now. I'm very tired.
Still seated, SUSANAH *watches.*

THOMAS: Good night. I'll be in in a minute.
THOMAS *stands as* ANTHONY *crosses away.* SUSANAH
watches as the distance between them grows. Then
ANTHONY, *at the stage right edge, freezes, facing upstage*
while THOMAS, *at upstage left, turns away. They go into*
silhouette. Music plays in the background as SUSANAH
is isolated in a pool of light. Slowly, she faces out.

SUSANAH: Once . . . I remember a beach, and the three of us.
One of those islands—a little one—way off. We'd traveled together, like comrades, or musketeers, or stooges.
And the water was this strange, shocking blue. They
were in the shallows, Thomas and Anthony, throwing a
beach ball back and forth, and the sky was so bright it
seemed sort of exploding, the sun glaring down, and I
thought of snow. Looking up, I thought of the way it falls.
The way snow is cold and delicate, and yet it falls.

BLACKOUT
END OF ACT ONE

ACT TWO

Dreamy light. ANTHONY *wanders. Music plays in the background. Almost limping, he makes his way out onto the upstage left edge. A phone begins to ring. Lights up on* DR. CHAPMAN's *table and phone. The phone rings again and then* DR. CHAPMAN, *wearing his pajamas, comes running out from downstage left. He crosses the apron to the phone and picks it up.*

DR. CHAPMAN: Hello.
   ANTHONY *is in a pool of light.*

ANTHONY: Dr. Chapman, hello?

DR. CHAPMAN: Anthony. Hello.

ANTHONY: Hello.

DR. CHAPMAN: Are you all right?

ANTHONY: So-so. I'm so-so.

DR. CHAPMAN: What time is it? It's the middle of the night. Where are you?

ANTHONY: I'm in our living room.

DR. CHAPMAN: Goodness—it's almost—it's nearly four in the morning.

ANTHONY: Is it? Did I wake you?

DR. CHAPMAN: Well, yes. But that's all right. Couldn't you sleep?

ANTHONY: You have become my friend in such a short time, Robert. You will be there for me, won't you. You have not run away. I was afraid that you had. But I know that's not true. You will keep your promise.

DR. CHAPMAN: What I have promised, Anthony, I will do.

ANTHONY: Because you are my angel now. Do you know that? You are the angel my prayers searched for and found. But I must ask you for something more. Are you listening?

DR. CHAPMAN: Yes.

ANTHONY: I must ask you to help Thomas too. We must find a way to help him, a way to protect him. Will you do that?

DR. CHAPMAN: I really think you should try and get some sleep now, Anthony. Does Thomas know you're up?

ANTHONY: Will you do it, though? Will you help him? You know I'm right.

DR. CHAPMAN: Yes. I'll try.

ANTHONY: I am tired.

DR. CHAPMAN: Of course you are. All right, then. Good night. (*He speaks again, insisting.*) Good night, Anthony.

ANTHONY: Good night, Dr. Chapman.

They hang up. As DR. CHAPMAN *puts the phone down, he looks out.*

DR. CHAPMAN: An "angel" he calls me. An "angel." Well, maybe. (*He begins to change from his pajamas into a shirt, shoes, his suit.*) I know what he wants. It's a prayer, really. His prayer. Deliver him. Intercede. Give him the relief he needs. Fly to him, and with my bag of pharmaceutical tricks perform a miracle. Well, maybe. He calls to me, and I think, Is it really miracles that I bring? Well, maybe. Almost. Once I was to be his "instrument." Now I am his "angel." At first glance two very different things. And yet I'm wondering, Are they so different? Are they really so different? What both do, finally, is work the will of another. Some superior other? Both are in fact more or less useless until they're moved, until they are directed. So they're servants, really. Slaves, actually. And yet they share an appealing trait—a wondrous trait—one that I want, because of the way it will place me outside the compunctions and strictures holding me in. Such common human cares would have no meaning were I an instrument—no meaning were I an angel. (*He is in his suit now, facing out.*)
As the one, I will be inanimate and mindless, and so completely unbothered by our moral fuss. As the other, as the angel, I will be supernatural. I will occupy a privileged realm beyond all recrimination.
He turns now and faces up center. ANTHONY *is revealed dressed in a suit. He stands near the couch and coffee table, holding a tray with water, pills, a glass.*

DR. CHAPMAN: I will act from a place indifferent to reproach, no matter what I do, no matter how cataclysmic my deeds. (*He walks toward* ANTHONY.)

ANTHONY: I'm ready. I'm ready now. I'm doing it.

DR. CHAPMAN: I know.
   As they settle on the couch at the table:

DR. CHAPMAN: It's time. You're right. (*He spreads the pills on the table.*)

ANTHONY: I'm ready. I'm ready. I really am. (*He drinks, but he is clearly taking in too much water.*) See! (*He drinks again.*) See!

DR. CHAPMAN: Anthony! No, no. That's not the way.

ANTHONY: It is. It's what you taught me. It's what you did.

DR. CHAPMAN (*Worried*): No.

ANTHONY: It is.

DR. CHAPMAN: No.
   ANTHONY *drinks again, clearly taking too much water, and* DR. CHAPMAN *reaches to physically stop him.*

DR. CHAPMAN: Stop! No, no, you're drinking too much water. You'll fill up too quickly, Anthony. It won't work.

ANTHONY: I'm sorry. I'm sorry. I thought I was doing what you said.

DR. CHAPMAN: No, no. Not at all.

ANTHONY: Show me, then. Show me. You do it, you show me.

DR. CHAPMAN: All right.

ANTHONY: You do it. Show me the way to do it.
As ANTHONY *pours the pills into* DR. CHAPMAN'*s hand and hands him the water:*

DR. CHAPMAN: All right. (*The water already in his hand, he takes a pill.*) Now watch.

ANTHONY: Yes.

DR. CHAPMAN (*Mincingly, he takes a pill.*): There. See.

ANTHONY: No. That's not how you do it.

DR. CHAPMAN: Yes. (*Mincingly, he takes another pill.*) Watch.

ANTHONY: No, no. You do it like this.
ANTHONY *raises a handful of pills to his mouth, jams them in, and gulps.*

ANTHONY: Quickly. We don't have much time.
Raising a handful to his mouth, DR. CHAPMAN *does as instructed. He takes the pills, drinks, and begins gulping and coughing.*

ANTHONY: Yes, yes. Do a few more. You need a few more.
As DR. CHAPMAN *takes more pills and drinks:*

ANTHONY: That's right. Good. Faster. Just a few more.
Growing sluggish, DR. CHAPMAN *turns to* ANTHONY.

DR. CHAPMAN: No. (*trying to offer the pills and water to* ANTHONY) You. You.

ANTHONY (*shoving the pills back*): No. You.
Music plays in the background, weird, groaning, spooky.

DR. CHAPMAN (*taking more pills*): I'll die.

ANTHONY: No, no.

DR. CHAPMAN (*growing dizzy, slurring*): I will. You're killing me.

ANTHONY: No, no. (*rising, a needle and bottle in his hand*) Nooo. Here's the syringe.

DR. CHAPMAN: You are. You're killing me. Don't you see what you're doing?
ANTHONY *draws the morphine and squirts a tiny spray into the air.*

ANTHONY: Shhhhhhhhhhhh.

DR. CHAPMAN: Anthony.

ANTHONY: No. (*He hands the needle to* DR. CHAPMAN.)

DR. CHAPMAN: What? What? (*injecting the drug into his own arm*) What? I don't know what. I'm . . . I'm . . .

ANTHONY: Let yourself go. Let yourself go.

DR. CHAPMAN (*sagging backward*): Let yourself go, Anthony.

ANTHONY: Let yourself go, Anthony. Let yourself go.

DR. CHAPMAN: Go. Please, Anthony. Please. Go, go.

ANTHONY: Are you feeling woozy, Dr. Chapman?

DR. CHAPMAN: Don't ask me that, don't ask me that, don't ask me.

ANTHONY: I think you are. I am.

DR. CHAPMAN: No. No. Not woozy. Not woozy.
The thunderous jangle of an alarm clock fills the air, and
DR. CHAPMAN *bolts up, screaming.*

DR. CHAPMAN (*Screaming, he awakens from a nightmare.*):
Agggggggggggggghhhhhh!
On the screen we see projected: FEBRUARY 1, 1990.
Lights up on the DOORMAN, *who stands reading a*
newspaper, a phone to his ear.

DOORMAN: That's what they're saying. It's right here in black
and white. The trade rumors are rampant. Mike and the
Mad Dog are incensed! Buy it yourself, if you don't believe me, Bobby, it's on the newsstand. You got a nearby
newsstand, right? Read the damn story and then argue
with me if you want to.
As DR. CHAPMAN *strides across the apron toward him:*

DOORMAN: I gotta go. (*Hanging up, stepping in front of* DR.
CHAPMAN.) Doc, Doc, I'm sorry, but that ticket thing isn't
going to work out. I got carried away, you know. I
thought this guy was somebody I could count on—he has
a season pass, he sells them when he can't go. He's sold
the rest of the goddamn season to some total stranger.
So I'm sorry to disappoint you. Maybe we could just get
together and watch a game on TV.
As DR. CHAPMAN *moves on past the* DOORMAN, *heading*
for the upstage left corner of the platform:

DOORMAN: If you're mad at me, I don't blame you, Doc. But
TV could be fun! You think it over.
Lights up on THOMAS, ANTHONY, *and* SUSANAH; *the three*
of them are disturbed.

SUSANAH: Yes, but what did he say?

THOMAS: He sounded distraught.

ANTHONY: But what did he say?

THOMAS: He had to see us.

ANTHONY: Has something gone wrong?

THOMAS: He didn't say. He just said he had to see us.
    The doorbell rings. SUSANAH *runs to open the door, and*
    DR. CHAPMAN *steps in.*

SUSANAH: Dr. Chapman, how are you?

DR. CHAPMAN: All right.

THOMAS: You gave me quite a scare. What's wrong? Is there
    something wrong?

DR. CHAPMAN: No, no.

ANTHONY: You're sure.

THOMAS: Would you like a cup of tea? Or coffee?

DR. CHAPMAN: No.

THOMAS: I have some coffee cake. I didn't bake it myself, but—

DR. CHAPMAN: I'll have some coffee.

THOMAS: All right. Good. (*He heads for the kitchen.*)

DR. CHAPMAN: It's too soon!

THOMAS (*freezing, turning back*): What?

DR. CHAPMAN: It's too soon. February tenth is too soon.

SUSANAH: Something's happened and you're not telling us.

DR. CHAPMAN: No, no, I just don't think Anthony's ready. I don't think you're ready, Anthony.

ANTHONY: Why do you say that? What's happened? I am prepared.

DR. CHAPMAN: Then answer me one question. I have one question! If you're so prepared, why haven't you done it already?

THOMAS: What?

ANTHONY: Something's happened. Susanah, make him tell us what's happened.

SUSANAH: None of us know exactly what it is you're saying, Dr. Chapman. Could you be a little more—

DR. CHAPMAN: Why hasn't he done it? Why have you chosen such an unreliable method, Anthony? There are guns. Go to a store that sells hunting equipment. You can walk out with a shotgun. That'll do it. That's been proven. Or rent a car. Go to Hertz, and then drive it off a cliff.

THOMAS: You're not serious. (*To* SUSANAH.) He's not serious, is he?

DR. CHAPMAN: I'm very serious. And I'm asking him to be serious. I'm asking Anthony to think honestly about why he has chosen a method that is so uncertain when there are other ways.

ANTHONY: I am not a violent person, Dr. Chapman.

DR. CHAPMAN: You're not a violent person, but you want to kill yourself.

ANTHONY: I couldn't do such things to myself.

DR. CHAPMAN: That's my point, Anthony. You're making my point. Look at how you keep worrying about Thomas. You're still so attached to him. Is that the behavior of someone who wants to die?

THOMAS: I knew it. I knew it. I knew that's what you were getting around to. I'm the obstruction—I'm the—

DR. CHAPMAN: No! But you're unreliable! And the whole thing—everything we've considered is very, very—I mean, lies will be necessary, but you won't be able to tell them, Thomas. You won't.

ANTHONY (*pulling a vial from his pocket, presenting it*): I have the Levo-Dromoran tablets, Robert, see. Like you asked of me. Remember? I did just as you asked at the clinic.

THOMAS: I said I'd make some coffee, but I didn't. (*He starts off.*)

DR. CHAPMAN (*taking the pill vial, settling on the couch*): I'll take a cup.

SUSANAH: Me too.

ANTHONY: I performed at the clinic just as you asked, Dr. Chapman. I laughed and joked. I spoke only of the future and only of my determination to fight. I think I was a little bit clichéd and sentimental. But they gave them to me. You said that would mean they suspect nothing. I passed the test. We have nothing to fear from them.

DR. CHAPMAN (*holding the pills*): I have an alternative.

ANTHONY: An alternative to what, Robert?

DR. CHAPMAN: To these. To the pills. Anthony—you could simply stop eating and you could stop drinking, and then you would—in just days you would—

SUSANAH (*calling off*): Thomas, I think you should come in here!

ANTHONY: Wait, wait, let him finish.

THOMAS (*from off*): Be right there!

DR. CHAPMAN: This would be legal. It would not take long—only a few days, and you would be dead.

ANTHONY: From what?

DR. CHAPMAN: Of starvation. Of dehydration.
    As THOMAS *comes in with a tray of coffee, cups, saucers:*

SUSANAH: He's telling Anthony to starve himself to death.

THOMAS: What?

SUSANAH: That if he just didn't eat or drink for several days, he would die of starvation. It would be legal.

Thomas: That's insane. Isn't it? (*to* Anthony) Or do you think you could do that?

Dr. Chapman: His condition is so weak already that it would only be a matter of a short time—a few days and then, well—

Anthony: But I would be awake, wouldn't I? Is that what you're saying? I would just sit there for days and—no, no—is that what you're saying? For hour after hour, saying, "No, I will not eat, I will not drink."

Thomas: And we would what? We would just sit here and watch him starve to death?

Dr. Chapman: I see you, Anthony—and life comes out of you still—even now—so much life.

Anthony: I pray for it to be over, Dr. Chapman. I pray for it.

Dr. Chapman: I'm telling you a way. I'm telling you—

Anthony: No. No, we had the date, we'd worked out most of the details, I thought. What happened to you?

Dr. Chapman: Nothing.

Anthony: No, no, something happened.

Dr. Chapman: I went to sleep and . . .

Anthony: Yes.

Dr. Chapman: And I was sleeping and . . .

Thomas: Yes.

SUSANAH: What?

ANTHONY: What? (*Facing* DR. CHAPMAN.)

DR. CHAPMAN: You don't want the gun. You don't want the knife or car. Not the crazy jump off the bridge.

ANTHONY (*hopeful*): No.

DR. CHAPMAN: Do you know why? So it's familiar—just taking a pill—like taking an aspirin, or a decongestant, or an antibiotic.

ANTHONY: Yes.

DR. CHAPMAN: And then sleep.

ANTHONY (*pleased that* DR. CHAPMAN *is getting it*): Yes.

DR. CHAPMAN: So it's all familiar and gentle.

ANTHONY: Yes.

DR. CHAPMAN: No violence. No death, even, really. Just a pill and then sleep. A trick and then sleep. So it's civilized.

ANTHONY: Yes! Do you know why I think we're having this conversation, Robert? What it means? I think we have left too much unclear. Too much has not been agreed upon by us all. The plan is not precise enough, Robert. (*Suddenly exhausted, latching onto* DR. CHAPMAN.) I think we need to work it all out, every detail exactly. So we know. Then it will be easier to accept. I know I have questions. We all must.
With DR. CHAPMAN's *assistance,* ANTHONY *makes his way to the couch.*

ANTHONY: Let's do that. I want to do that. We will know then that there can be no retreat. It must be at night. That's the first thing I know. With absolute, with perfect certainty, it must be in the dark. Do you all agree?

DR. CHAPMAN: I'm exhausted. (*He settles in the stage left chair, takes off his coat.*)

ANTHONY: We have the date, and it must be at night. Is there any need to change it, Dr. Chapman? Is there any need to change the date?

DR. CHAPMAN: No.

ANTHONY: Then what I want first, in the late part of the day, is to spend some time with my friends, with Susanah and Thomas. A dinner, a last dinner together. That's another thing about which I'm certain. Is there a problem with that, Dr. Chapman?

DR. CHAPMAN: Well, yes, there is. You can't really eat anything, Anthony. You know, the pills. You don't want to throw up the food, and so—

ANTHONY: Of course not, no, no.

SUSANAH: Of course he couldn't—we'd be careful. (*Moves in, sits down.*)

ANTHONY: But I can sit with them. Spend time with them.

DR. CHAPMAN: Yes.

ANTHONY: That would be all right. The two of us first, Thomas and myself alone, and then the three of us.
    DR. CHAPMAN *is nodding.*

THOMAS: Maybe we shouldn't have any dinner. (*Moves in, sitting on the couch with* ANTHONY.)

ANTHONY: No, no, I want it. A dinner table fully set, with candles and our plates we brought from France. And then the music, Dr. Chapman, and the slides.

DR. CHAPMAN: That's up to you.

ANTHONY: I want it. But it must all be set up for me. The music, the Bach, and the slides of my life, so that I can watch them, the slides of my friends and loved ones set up to project. I won't be able to set the projector up.

SUSANAH: No, no, of course not. We understand that.

ANTHONY: Will that be all right, Dr. Chapman?

DR. CHAPMAN: It doesn't matter to me.

ANTHONY: Thomas and I will spend the day together, and then Susanah could join us. We will dine together, and say goodbye. (*He sags and lies down, his head on* THOMAS's *lap.*)

SUSANAH: I'll help with the slides and the music. I'll make certain they're all prepared.

DR. CHAPMAN (*nodding*): All right. Yes.

SUSANAH: Thomas and I have had a kind of preliminary discussion of some of this, and what we were thinking is that maybe we should go out of town. After dinner, when we leave here. We would take the train. We have friends in Princeton.

THOMAS: We've friends at the university there.

ANTHONY: What time would this be?

THOMAS: We haven't settled that.

SUSANAH: But we could spend the night there.

DR. CHAPMAN: The timetable must be very strict.

THOMAS: Yes.

SUSANAH: Yes.

ANTHONY: We all know that.

DR. CHAPMAN: Your departure would have to be locked in at a somewhat early hour—say, five-thirty. And once we agree on a timetable, that timetable has to be inflexible, so that we all know exactly where we should be and what we should be doing when Anthony starts taking the pills. If you knew, Anthony, that you were to start at six o'clock—what time would you want Thomas and Susanah to leave you? That's what I'm asking. How long would you need alone before you started?

ANTHONY: I don't know.

DR. CHAPMAN: You'll need some time alone, I would think.

ANTHONY (*sitting back up*): Yes.

DR. CHAPMAN: To make the transition. Before you start. Let's say they were to leave at five-thirty—that would mean an early dinner at four.

ANTHONY: Is that all right?

THOMAS: It's fine with me.

SUSANAH: Thomas would be here; I could arrive a little before that. Say three-thirty.

ANTHONY: All right, then. Three-thirty.

DR. CHAPMAN: So then they'll be gone by—you'll have to be gone by five-thirty. At six P.M. Anthony will turn on the slides and he will turn on the music and he will begin to take the pills. Six o'clock sharp. There can be no variation.

ANTHONY: So I would be alone for one half hour. For my transition.

DR. CHAPMAN: Yes.

ANTHONY: It is maybe too long. What do you think?

DR. CHAPMAN: Well, you could start at five-forty-five.

ANTHONY: I could. Yes. But—no—let's keep it at six.

DR. CHAPMAN: You're sure.

ANTHONY: Yes. Six.

DR. CHAPMAN: And you must take the pills as we've practiced. Slowly, methodically. Little sips.

ANTHONY: Yes.

DR. CHAPMAN: Then at eight-thirty, I will let myself in. Someone will have given me a key. I will have the morphine.

ANTHONY: So you have decided, Robert. No longer can you say
you have not decided, because you have, haven't you.

DR. CHAPMAN: Yes.
In a sudden spot of light, DR. CHAPMAN *sits, brooding,*
thinking.

DR. CHAPMAN: He's right. But when did I decide? I can't lo-
cate that clear point where I decide to do it—to find him
holding on for dear life and then to simply nudge him
over the edge. Or did it just happen? Was it not so much
a matter of—
By now the lights have lifted to include the others and
they are staring at DR. CHAPMAN.

SUSANAH: Dr. Chapman?

DR. CHAPMAN: What? *(Startled, looking at them.)* Sorry. When
I arrive, I'll go to the bedroom and stay only long enough
to make certain that Anthony is dead. If he's not, I'll use
the morphine; I'll inject the morphine. If he is dead, I'll
leave without doing anything. I won't notify anyone.

THOMAS: So we won't know what happened?

DR. CHAPMAN: Either way, he will be dead. But you'll have to
come back and find out, as if you had no idea.
THOMAS *rises and strides toward the kitchen.*

DR. CHAPMAN: Thomas? Are you following this?
THOMAS *stops.*

THOMAS (*turning back to them*): Yes, yes. Just—just ignore me, please. We've agreed I should be ignored.

SUSANAH (*moving to* THOMAS): You're doing fine, Thomas.

ANTHONY: Go on, Robert.

DR. CHAPMAN (*rising, approaching* THOMAS): Are you all right, Thomas? I want you to tell me if you're not.

THOMAS: Can't you just ignore me? Can't you just do that? (*Turns to* SUSANAH.) Tell him to ignore me.

SUSANAH: Don't worry about Thomas, Dr. Chapman, I'll make sure that he—

DR. CHAPMAN: No. I have to be certain you're following what I'm saying, Thomas, and that you're in full agreement. By noon the next day, you and Susanah will return and discover the body and call the clinic.

THOMAS: They'll send a doctor, won't they, whoever we tell?

DR. CHAPMAN: They'll have to, and then it will be up to him, to this doctor, to pronounce death. This will be a highly critical, highly precarious moment for us all, the time that he is here with the two of you. If he starts asking questions, just remember that you were out of town. You know nothing. If he gets suspicious and demands an autopsy, you will have to resort to the codicil in Anthony's will requesting that there be no autopsy. That should stop him.

SUSANAH: Do you think it will?

DR. CHAPMAN: It's really all we can do. They should respect it and remove the deceased.

ANTHONY: And then what?

DR. CHAPMAN: You mean after they take the body—your body— away? (*Returning to his chair, sitting.*) Well, that should be the end of it. If it all goes well, that should be the end of it. All right? Does everyone understand? Are we clear?

THOMAS (*moving off toward the kitchen*): Yes.

SUSANAH (*following* THOMAS): Yes.
    ANTHONY *sits watching as* THOMAS *and* SUSANAH *start to walk away.*

ANTHONY: Maybe we should go over it one more time.

THOMAS: It's dizzying, really. I feel like—I mean, actually I never felt anything like this before, ever. I don't know what this feeling is.

ANTHONY: Thomas and I will spend the day together and say good-bye.

DR. CHAPMAN: At four o'clock, Susanah, you will—

SUSANAH: No, no. I said three-thirty. I will arrive at three-thirty and we will dine together, the three of us will dine together.

ANTHONY: But I won't eat.

SUSANAH: No, you won't eat. At five-thirty Thomas and I will go to Princeton to spend the night.

DR. CHAPMAN: At six P.M.—Anthony?

ANTHONY: I will start to take the pills. And I will do as I've been instructed until, well—

DR. CHAPMAN: At eight-thirty I will let myself into the apartment. I will check Anthony, and if he isn't dead I will use the morphine, and I will not notify anyone. If he is dead, I will not use the morphine, and I will not notify anyone. At noon the next day, Thomas and Susanah will return to discover the body and call the clinic. The doctor who comes to pronounce death will ask questions, maybe demand an autopsy. If he does . . .

SUSANAH: We hope and pray the codicil to Anthony's will will stop him.

DR. CHAPMAN: Yes, and—

ANTHONY: You forgot about the slides.

DR. CHAPMAN: I did?

ANTHONY: You forgot about the music—the Bach—and the slides.

THOMAS: You're right. But we'll see to it.

ANTHONY: It's very important. I won't be able to do it alone.

SUSANAH: We know that. Sorry, Anthony.

THOMAS: Sorry.

SUSANAH: We're sorry.

> *Lights go to black, except for on* DR. CHAPMAN *and* AN-
> THONY. DR. CHAPMAN *is still seated on the chair in a pool
> of faint light.* ANTHONY *is seated in the opposite chair,
> but he is lit in a ghostly way, as if he isn't really there.
> Music plays in the background.*

DR. CHAPMAN (*thinking, brooding, speaking*): Primitive people
saw death less certainly, less categorically, as the enemy,
than we do. For them, the rock, the flower, the tree, the
deer, the buffalo, the bird, the rain all had souls animat-
ing them. In their world, everything possessed soul and
so it was plentiful, soul was plentiful.

> *He takes a tie from his pocket, buttons his collar, and
> puts the tie on, as he continues.*

DR. CHAPMAN: They were members of a tribe—they were
participants in the tribe—it was not an affiliation but an
interior, essential aspect of themselves. When they passed
away, the tribe lived on. With the cessation of their life
as human beings, they returned to the world of the great
spirit hovering all around them in everything in a vast
embrace that held all of nature within it, that embodied
all of nature. It's a belief far different from our modern
faith, in which we are unique, individual egos. A far cry
from our Christian concept in which death is a wrench-
ing that rips us away from the only living thing we know,
our bodies. Our grave sites are dark holes, dark cells in
which we are deposited and contained, walled off from
nature and from one another, encased in caskets that, like
our egos, isolate us as we wait to be recalled through the
doctrine of the Resurrection, whose stipulations condemn
us to live forever as our desperate singular selves.

> *A phone rings. On the screen we see the projection:
> FEBRUARY 8, 1990.*

Lights up in the apartment as ANTHONY *is hobbling to the phone, which he picks up.*

ANTHONY: Hello. . . . Oh, yes, Thomas. Hello. . . . No, no. It's fine. That's fine. Don't worry about it. As soon as you can, but don't worry about it. . . . Robert is here. We're just talking. See you soon. . . . Yes. Bye-bye. (*He hangs up and moves back toward* DR. CHAPMAN.)

DR. CHAPMAN: Where are they?

ANTHONY: Having fun. Feeling guilty. Did you wear that tie intentionally, Robert?

DR. CHAPMAN: What?

ANTHONY: That tie.
As DR. CHAPMAN *looks down at the tie:*

ANTHONY: It's the tie you wore the first day you came here.

DR. CHAPMAN: Is it? Really?

ANTHONY: You didn't know?

DR. CHAPMAN: I wore this on the first day I came here?

ANTHONY: I thought you probably didn't know.

DR. CHAPMAN: Really? You're sure.

ANTHONY: I have an affinity for such tidbits.

DR. CHAPMAN: I had no idea. I just put it on.

ANTHONY: Is such a thing possibly an accident?

DR. CHAPMAN: I don't know. I do not know.

ANTHONY: Do you suppose? What do you think?
DR. CHAPMAN *looks up from his tie. He shrugs, gesturing his helpless ignorance of many things.*

DR. CHAPMAN: Will Thomas be back soon?

ANTHONY: He said he was on his way home as soon as he hung up. Why?

DR. CHAPMAN: I feel like going. I want to be gone before he arrives. Before he and Susanah arrive. I don't want to talk anymore. I'm sorry. Do you understand?

ANTHONY: I have no desire to talk either. I really, truly don't.

DR. CHAPMAN: Will you be all right alone for a few minutes? (*Glancing at his watch.*)

ANTHONY: Are you tired?

DR. CHAPMAN: I am.
He rises and heads for his overcoat, which lies on an upstage chair.

ANTHONY: I'm very tired; but then I'm always tired. I'll walk you to the door.

DR. CHAPMAN: You don't have to.

ANTHONY: I think I do. (*But he can't, and he sags back down on the chair.*)

ANTHONY: I'm concerned that because of the diarrhea my body will not absorb the barbiturate. Am I right to worry?

As DR. CHAPMAN *returns, carrying his coat:*

ANTHONY: I've seen more and more undigested tablets—potassium tablets—in my stool. They go right through my system. (*Rising to face* DR. CHAPMAN.) The barbiturates could do the same thing, couldn't they, and just go through me?

DR. CHAPMAN: Don't worry. Don't worry, Anthony.
   DR. CHAPMAN *drops his coat.* ANTHONY *bends to retrieve it.*

DR. CHAPMAN: Let me get it.

ANTHONY: No.
   ANTHONY *picks up the coat and holds it for* DR. CHAPMAN *to slip into.*

DR. CHAPMAN: Don't worry.

ANTHONY: Without you, I must worry.

DR. CHAPMAN: We have the pills, a hundred and ten of the pills. Half would be enough. I have the morphine and the syringe.

ANTHONY: You swear. You swear you will be there for me.

DR. CHAPMAN: I'll be there.

ANTHONY: From my soul, I thank you.
   He reaches and hugs DR. CHAPMAN, *a strong, simple embrace that* DR. CHAPMAN *returns, patting* ANTHONY *on the shoulder. They stand like this and then they part.* DR. CHAPMAN *nods and starts toward the door.*

ANTHONY (*pulling a key from his robe pocket*): Here is the key you are to use.

DR. CHAPMAN (*faltering, stepping back*): Oh, yes. The key.

ANTHONY: It's my key.
  Taking the key, DR. CHAPMAN *starts to the door. Then he stops and looks back.*

DR. CHAPMAN: I'll see you on Saturday.

ANTHONY: Yes. But I won't see you.
  Loud blast of a radio: the SPORTSCASTER's *voice, the sounds of a hockey game. The* DOORMAN *gazes up, listening.*

VOICE OF SPORTSCASTER: With a two-man disadvantage, the Rangers are scrambling to protect their one-goal lead, while the Red Wings apply the pressure as they bring the puck up the ice and Rankowski fires a long blast.

DOORMAN: WHAT ARE THEY DOING! WHAT ARE THEY DOING?
  As DR. CHAPMAN *approaches:*

DOORMAN: It's torture, Doc. They're torturin' me. I only want the best for them, don't I? I want 'em to win. Isn't that what they want? Isn't that what they've devoted their lives to? Winning? So why don't they do it?
  DR. CHAPMAN *is staring at the* DOORMAN.

DR. CHAPMAN: Oh. Eddie.

DOORMAN: What'sa matter, Doc, is something wrong? You look like something's wrong?

DR. CHAPMAN: No, no. Why?

DOORMAN: You don't look like yourself, Doc. What is it?
    DR. CHAPMAN *turns out, isolated in a pool of light, while
the* DOORMAN *stands a few yards off in a different pool
of fading light. Music plays in the background.*

DR. CHAPMAN: He knows me. How could I have forgotten? He's
seen me come and go, and our conversations have a dis-
torted importance to him, and so he will remember. And
yet I forgot. How could I? And yet I did. Is this forget-
ting like the act of putting on a certain tie on a certain
day? A simple gesture of enormous effect performed from
within perfect ignorance. (*He storms across the apron to
his phone and table.*) More and more I feel like a criminal. And yet Anthony demands that I go on. He haunts
me with the remnant of his smile. But I am haunted in
other ways, too. Simple things, ordinary things. Like this
moment with Eddie. Once his greetings were a pointless
pleasure, but now—now! The doorman knows me! The
doorman knows me! And all this occurs in anticipation
of the deed. How far will this poison spread once the time
has come and passed and Anthony is in fact dead? What
will become of my life? Will anything ordinary be left?

On the screen is projected: FEBRUARY 9, 1990.
    The phone in DR. CHAPMAN's *apartment rings. He
snatches it up.*

DR. CHAPMAN: Yes!

SUSANAH: Dr. Chapman, this is Susanah. We need to speak to
you.
    The lights rise on the opposite side of the stage. SUSANAH
is at the Beacon diner. THOMAS *sits at the table with coffee. She is at a nearby pay phone.*

DR. CHAPMAN: What?

SUSANAH: Susanah Tomkins.

DR. CHAPMAN: What's happened?

SUSANAH: We need to speak to you. Thomas and I. We're at an
all-night diner—the Beacon. It's near you. Thomas says
you know it.

DR. CHAPMAN: I do. Yes. What happened?

SUSANAH: You must come over. Can you come over?

DR. CHAPMAN: Actually, I'm in bed.

SUSANAH: Listen to me, Doctor. Come over. I know now why
I was brought into this situation—what I am to do. And
I think you know, too, don't you.

DR. CHAPMAN: No.

SUSANAH: I think you do. How soon can you get here?

DR. CHAPMAN: Twenty minutes, I would say. Approximately.
SUSANAH *hangs up.* DR. CHAPMAN *hangs up. Lights rise on*
THOMAS *at the table.* SUSANAH *strides up.*

SUSANAH: He's coming right over.

THOMAS (*sipping his coffee*): What did he say?

SUSANAH: That he'd be right over.

THOMAS: I hope he just does it. I hope he doesn't try to make us think it all through again. I can't think anymore. I can't do it.

SUSANAH: You're doing fine, Thomas.

THOMAS: But I can't think anymore. I used to think that thinking went somewhere. That it, you know, progressed. That a person could think their way from one point to another.

SUSANAH: Well, that's what we would all like to believe, I guess.

THOMAS: And I'm not doing fine. How can you say I'm doing fine?

SUSANAH: Can I be honest? It's the fullness of your feelings for Anthony; they are just in some way overwhelming you. And I think there's a way in which you're very naive, too, Thomas. I mean, we've discussed that. It's not that you can't think, so much as the fact that your thoughts are trying to rise through these big stormy waves that are drowning out the thoughts you are having.

THOMAS: I don't feel like I'm thinking.

SUSANAH: When a person loves someone as much as you love Anthony, they want to give them what they want. Especially when that person is in such desperate circumstances. But watching you and caring about you the way I do, I can't blind myself to the distress you're in.

THOMAS: I'm ashamed of what we're doing.

SUSANAH: And what does that accomplish? Fine. Be ashamed. Good. Go ahead. Take your time. But what does it accomplish?

THOMAS: I don't know. I don't think it's supposed to be purposeful. I mean, utilitarian.

SUSANAH: Anthony has always charmed you, he's even manipulated you. I mean, not cruelly or to your disadvantage, but still he's done it to get his way. I've never doubted that he loved you. But he always wanted his way, and you didn't seem to care.

THOMAS: Sometimes I did.

SUSANAH: Sometimes, sure. But not most of the time.

THOMAS: No. It was fun.

SUSANAH: But this isn't fun, is it. And, of course, the point is that he has a right to choose to die if he wants to, but not to involve you beyond what you can tolerate. Beyond what you can live with. So there's really no choice.

THOMAS: I pray sometimes at night. On and on for hours, sometimes. Like I did as a child. Anthony sleeps. I can't sleep and he sleeps. I don't want him to die.

SUSANAH: There are limits to love. We—by who we are— define those limits.

THOMAS: I looked over the other night and he was so peaceful, the way he was sleeping. He had what he wants. I started praying to God, you know, saying that if His mind is made up—if God's mind is made up to kill Anthony—I was praying—begging, actually—that He should just hurry up and do it.

SUSANAH *looks up as* DR. CHAPMAN *enters and moves toward them.*

THOMAS *looks and watches* DR. CHAPMAN *cross the remaining few yards between them.*

DR. CHAPMAN: What? What is it?

THOMAS: Thank you for coming, Dr. Chapman.

DR. CHAPMAN (*sitting*): Susanah didn't really give me any choice.

SUSANAH: You're going to get caught.

DR. CHAPMAN: What are you talking about?

THOMAS: You know you are. We all know it.

DR. CHAPMAN: Why do you say that? Has something happened?

SUSANAH: We're just facing facts.

THOMAS: It'll never work.

SUSANAH: None of us wants to do this. We never have. We've only tried to do it for Anthony.

THOMAS: I was honest about that with you right from the beginning.

DR. CHAPMAN: But we've worked everything out. I thought we had a plan that was satisfactory to everyone.

THOMAS: Susanah contacted the Hemlock Society.

SUSANAH: I talked to a legal consultant there. He's very sympathetic to these things. He studies these things, and in his opinion we have no chance.

DR. CHAPMAN: Are you sure who he is? How did you meet him?

SUSANAH: No, no. I went there. I went to their chapter. And according to their legal consultant the whole idea of preventing the autopsy doesn't have a chance. It's a fantasy. By New York law, the newly dead must be held for forty-eight hours before cremation. The odds are almost one hundred percent that someone in the coroner's office will examine the body. And because of our circumstances, because of an almost automatic suspicion of suicide in such a situation as this one, the coroner will order an autopsy. And once there's an autopsy, any injected substance will be discovered. They'll determine the time of death, and once they've done that, all they have to do is establish that you entered the building around that time. You will have been seen entering and leaving. The doorman knows you, doesn't he.

THOMAS: Did you forget that?

DR. CHAPMAN: No.

SUSANAH: When Thomas told me that, I was flabbergasted. What were you thinking?

THOMAS: He keeps telling me over and over how he knows you. What a great doctor you are.

SUSANAH: Once it comes out that you were in the apartment at that time, the obvious question for anyone to ask will be "Why?" Why should a doctor with almost no practice be present at the death of his one and only patient? Especially when the patient is known to be thinking about suicide? The answer to that question will bring the police to your door. They'll interrogate you, Dr. Chapman. They'll interrogate Thomas. They'll find out about me. We'll never manage it. How can we? We know nothing about coping in such circumstances—no, no, you're fired. You're fired, and that's that. There's no other way.

THOMAS: The key Anthony gave you—I know he gave you his key. So you could get in. You must give it back.
DR. CHAPMAN *stares.*

SUSANAH: Please, Dr. Chapman.

THOMAS: I could have tended him to the end, the most unbearable end—I could have cared for him no matter how awful it became. But I can't do this. I can't help kill him and then be forced to lie about it to the police—all the while knowing I've broken the law and I'm going to get caught.

SUSANAH: You must give us the key, Dr. Chapman.

DR. CHAPMAN: What about Anthony? I made him a promise.

SUSANAH: It's all right, Dr. Chapman. You're not part of this anymore. You really didn't want to get involved. You know you didn't. You're relieved to hear what we're saying. Just give in to it.
DR. CHAPMAN *takes the key from his pocket.*

DR. CHAPMAN: What will you tell Anthony?

SUSANAH: Nothing.

DR. CHAPMAN: Nothing?
    DR. CHAPMAN *slides the key across the table, and* THO-
    MAS *takes it.*

SUSANAH: We just won't tell him that you're not coming.

DR. CHAPMAN: The coward's way.

THOMAS: That's what we are, aren't we?

SUSANAH: But maybe it'll work. Maybe he'll die.
    The lights switch as THOMAS *and* DR. CHAPMAN *move
    away.* SUSANAH *stands in a pool of light, facing out.*

SUSANAH: My philosophy—if I can call it that—has always been
    more about the interpersonal moment. In other words,
    what are we doing? What can we do? These two men
    were my friends. Anthony was the dear one. I mean, the
    one who was a delight. He was fun and startling, the way
    he would come up with the precisely appropriate gesture
    that was somehow totally unexpected. But Thomas
    moved me more. And that's why I ended up doing what
    I did. At least, I think it is. There was Thomas, and he
    was going to live after all this, wasn't he? Did the ex-
    tremity of Anthony's circumstances eliminate every
    other concern? Was I wrong to side with the living? I
    know there are counterarguments, but in the version of
    the dispute I conducted within myself the conclusion
    seemed absolute. I had to protect Thomas. For the long-
    est time, I didn't know what I was to do, and I had the
    wisdom and patience not to act—not to be rash, but to
    wait until it came to me, until I knew the function I was
    to provide. And once I knew, I did it. It's my strength,
    really. It's my virtue. Anthony needed a protection I

couldn't grant. But what Thomas needed was within my reach. So I gave it.

She turns and exits.

THOMAS *enters with the pills, a pitcher of water, and a glass on a tray. He sets the tray down on the coffee table.*

ANTHONY *enters in a robe. He moves to the table and stands waiting, as* SUSANAH *enters with the slide projector, which she sets on the table beside the tray.*

ANTHONY *stands waiting.* SUSANAH *moves off to the side.* THOMAS *strides down right, facing out. He is alone in a sharp light.*

THOMAS: We actually went to a movie. In Princeton. The train makes a series of local stops. People get on and off at Newark and Metro Park and Metuchen. All different sizes and shapes of people. With everything hidden behind their eyes. The dinner the three of us shared was a weird, totally surreal experience. Susanah and me, trying to eat, while Anthony sipped water and stole glances at the clock. The three of us sitting there, trying to talk, saying good-bye. I thought about telling him that I could not permit things to go forward—I wanted to tell him that things had changed—but it seemed that if it was going to stop, he was the one to stop it. I kept sending him these messages with my eyes, to tell me what to do, looking at him for a sign that he was reconsidering, sifting his behavior for the slightest nuance of an invitation. It was like the first time that I kissed him. Who goes first? Should I? Shouldn't I? Then I was in a cab. The cab was on the street. Susanah was reading *Time* magazine, and somewhere in that interlude I started to imagine it all completed, all worked out. I imagined us returning to find him dead. It was hazy, a kind of cottony aftermath, the funeral, the tears. I imagined the crematorium and the fire—his ashes in a vase. I filled with love of him, and an unearthly sadness, and then I imagined myself eating the ashes. I imagined the spoon and I imagined the taste of the ashes in my mouth. Susanah, I realized, was staring into my eyes, and we were in fact on the train. I don't know what she saw. Our friends in Princeton wanted to go to a movie and have a late dinner. They met us at the station and we went straight to the movie. *Music starts. On the screen we see the projection: FEBRUARY 10, 1990.*

The music is the Pablo Casals recording of the 2nd Canon on the First Eight Bass Notes of the Aria Ground from Bach's "Goldberg" Variations. Variations 1, 2, 3, and 4.

ANTHONY *moves forward and sits down facing out. He turns on the projector, which flashes forward on automatic. Blink after blink.* ANTHONY *looks at the first slide, then he takes one pill, then a tiny sip. He shakes the pills out onto the tabletop. He pours some water into a glass. He lifts a pill to his lips and takes a little sip of water. He picks up another pill and takes another sip of water. Another pill and another. He looks at a slide. He rises, startled by the slide, staring. He sits back down and reaches forward to take up the pills, his lower lip trembling. He stops and sits there, shaking like a fevered child, and slowly, dutifully, his hands move to his mouth, bearing the pills, bearing the water. He takes another pill, growing sluggish now, his eyes drooping, his lips slack, his fingers clumsy. He tries to pick up a tablet, which he keeps knocking around the tabletop, unable to pluck it up. He pursues the tablet with his fingers, bumping it. And then his hand stops and he sits there, totally stupefied, eyes open, staring, dreaming for seconds. He tries to shake his head; he shakes his head slowly, like*

a man underwater. He breathes, taking in a deep, la-
bored breath. He looks down to find the pill and, as he
does, his head follows the angle of his eyes, slamming
down onto the tabletop, banging his nose. There is blood
slowly leaking from his nose and he wipes it over his face.
He presses his hand to the tabletop, seeking leverage, and
as he lifts himself into a tilted, awkward, upright posi-
tion, his other hand fumbles to lift the vial to his mouth
and dump it in. The pills spill out, some going in his
mouth, saliva and water dripping. He raises the glass and
tilts his head back, dumping the water over himself. He
loses his grip on the glass, grabs for it. It falls to the floor
and he falls after it, knocking the bottle over.

Nose bleeding, he kneels there, girding himself for
a final lunge to stand. But as he makes his move, he
has no balance. He has no strength; he topples side-
ways, pawing at the edge of the table but sinking onto
his side, his arm tangled beneath him. He can't stop
himself from falling, and he sinks down onto the floor
and lies there.

The music plays. The slides click on every ten sec-
onds. Blink, blink. The lights are fading. The seconds
tick by: ten, fifteen, twenty. His eyes flutter, slowly
close. The music plays and he lies there, and the lights
close down around him, darkening, darkening. The
music plays. ANTHONY *lies there. The music ends.*

On the screen we see projected: FEBRUARY 11, 1990.

THOMAS *and* SUSANAH *enter and stand in silhouette up-*
stage left, looking down. Slowly the lights rise on them.

THOMAS: Oh, God, oh, God.

SUSANAH: What do you think? Can you tell?

THOMAS: I don't know.

SUSANAH: We have to see. We have to be certain.

THOMAS (*moving forward, turning off the projector*): Ohh, this is so awful. Dammit.

SUSANAH: Oh, God. I think he's alive.

THOMAS: Are you sure?

SUSANAH: I don't know.
Moving close to ANTHONY, THOMAS *kneels and lifts* AN-THONY, *examining him, listening for a heartbeat.*

THOMAS: He's alive. He's alive.
A roar, a siren, a kind of chaos of noise cries through the air, growing louder. A phone starts to ring, the siren grows louder. A nurse/orderly sweeps through with a large broom, clearing the mess. Two paramedics rush a hospital bed onto the stage. The paramedics load ANTHONY *into the bed, attaching tubes and other appa-ratus. A large circular intensive-care isolation curtain lowers from the ceiling, along with a bright lamp. Then the sound of numerous respirators, each inhaling and exhaling at its own pace, increases in volume, a steady wet noise like the cascade from a fountain. At the same time,* THOMAS *and* DR. CHAPMAN *converge off to the side.*

THOMAS: I had to call the ambulance, didn't I? What else could I do?

DR. CHAPMAN: No, no, you did the right thing.

THOMAS: He was alive. Just lying there. It was so awful. He looked so awful.

DR. CHAPMAN: You had no choice.

THOMAS: He looked so desolate.

DR. CHAPMAN: You did the right thing.

THOMAS: They said he had to go into intensive care. They put him on a respirator. They pumped out his stomach and washed out his stomach and put him on a respirator. He is being fed intravenously. They said they didn't know if he was going to make it but they were going to try. It was preposterous!
THOMAS *wheels away, and* DR. CHAPMAN *turns, looking at* ANTHONY. *Slowly,* DR. CHAPMAN *makes his way to the bed. He stands, looking down. He pulls up a nearby chair and sits.*

DR. CHAPMAN: Anthony. (*Pause.*) Anthony, can you hear me?
ANTHONY *opens his eyes and looks up.*

DR. CHAPMAN: Can you see me, Anthony. Ahhh, yes. You know I wasn't there.
ANTHONY *stares at him. Because of the tube in his trachea, he can barely speak. He makes a sound.*

DR. CHAPMAN: Anthony, forgive me. Forgive us, if you can. But if you can't it's okay. I need to ask you some questions. Do you understand me?
ANTHONY, *his eyes alert, nods.*

DR. CHAPMAN: Now listen carefully. If you need anything repeated, I can do that. You have pneumonia. They can treat you for it. Or they can let you go. Do you understand? They can treat you, or they can let you go. Do you want to be treated for the pneumonia?

ANTHONY *stares, and then he nods yes.*

DR. CHAPMAN: You do. You want to be treated. Do you want
to live?
ANTHONY *stares, and then he nods yes.*

DR. CHAPMAN: All right. I'll tell them.
   DR. CHAPMAN *leans back in his chair, his hands to his
   head as he tries to understand what he has just heard.
   Then he moves back to* ANTHONY.

DR. CHAPMAN: You want to be treated. Do you still want to
die, Anthony?
ANTHONY *stares; he shakes his head no.*

DR. CHAPMAN *(patting* ANTHONY's *hand)*: I'll tell them.
   DR. CHAPMAN *rises, faces out.*

DR. CHAPMAN: I did what I said. I kept my word. I went to the
doctors immediately and made sure they understood
what Anthony had told me. I left no doubt about his
desire to live and urged them to labor to help him to the
utmost of their ability. They would do their best, they
told me, and as I looked into their eyes and listened to
their firm tones, I knew that for me at least the ordeal
was over. All our plans—the detail and chatter of our
effort to devise the proper action—to make it clear and
rational, our precious plan. And yet we'd ended up here.
What had we failed to take into account? It was simply
ourselves, and from ourselves had come betrayal. And
from our betrayal this moment. But what I did know was
that he was in their hands now, where he belonged. In
the care of the authorities, the experts, the true custodi-
ans. This strange dream was over for me, the trance
ended. We were back in the strong embrace of order,

nested in its rules. All my mistakes—and I saw clearly
that there had been many—all had failed to hurl me into
the rocks where I would have been broken.
*He turns and walks to the curtain and, taking hold of
it, he moves around the bed, closing the curtain around*
ANTHONY. *He strides out from behind the curtain and
downstage toward his table and phone.*

DR. CHAPMAN: I had come out safely, as much by accident, I
must admit, as by my own design. I was home, back in
my own life. And in the midst of my relief, I thought:
What next? The answer lay in my nephew. He of the
Christmas overcoat. (*Moving to center stage.*) A boy no
longer, he was now a grown man traveling in the city on
business. We met for dinner at the Golden Pavilion, a
small elegant Chinese restaurant. I stood at the window,
staring out into the clear crisp air, and the sturdy skyline of the city felt somehow fragile against the dark
vastness, the infinite and amazing night, and I thought—
Thunderous banging on door.

DR. CHAPMAN: What?
*Two men stride in from upstage, a plainclothes police-
man and a detective.*

DETECTIVE: Dr. Robert Chapman?

DR. CHAPMAN: Yes.

DETECTIVE: Hey, are you Chapman? We got a warrant for your
arrest.

DR. CHAPMAN: What? For what?

DETECTIVE: Put your coat on, sir.

DR. CHAPMAN: There must be some mistake.

COP (*grabbing* DR. CHAPMAN'*s coat from the chair, throwing it at him*): Put your coat on, Dr. Chapman.

DR. CHAPMAN: I don't understand.

COP: You have the right to remain silent. You have the right to an attorney.

DR. CHAPMAN: Wait a minute, wait a minute.

COP: Should you waive these rights, anything you say or do can and will be used against you. Do you understand these rights, Dr. Chapman?
The DOORMAN *strides on from downstage left.*

DOORMAN: He has no rights.

DR. CHAPMAN: Eddie!

COP: Do you wish to waive your rights?

DR. CHAPMAN: I don't understand what's happening here.

DETECTIVE: You're under arrest for the murder of Anthony Calderon.
Music plays in the background. Weird, spooky echoes, and wind, or breathing.

DR. CHAPMAN: Murder? But yesterday I saw him. He's in the— he's in the—ah, I can't think of the word. He's in the— ah—

DETECTIVE: Grave?

DR. CHAPMAN: No. Not the grave. He's in the I.C.E. No, it's not the I.C.E.
The cop grabs DR. CHAPMAN, *starts to force him off.*

COP: Trash ... dump?

DR. CHAPMAN: No. He wanted to live. He decided to live. He told me. He wanted to live.

DOORMAN (*marching up to* DR. CHAPMAN): Doctor, Doctor, how could you?

DR. CHAPMAN: Eddie, what are you doing here? You're a doorman.

DOORMAN: A man like you, Doctor!

DR. CHAPMAN: Wait a minute, I know where he is. It was a—there was a bed. And people—people were—

DETECTIVE: A morgue.

DR. CHAPMAN: No.

DOORMAN (*in* DR. CHAPMAN's *face*): Hockey? I wouldn't piss on you if your soul was on fire. That's him. He did it!

COP: It's time to go.
They start to drag DR. CHAPMAN *off toward the upstage left corner.*

DR. CHAPMAN: Wait. JUST WAIT! I'll think of it. Just wait! I'LL THINK OF WHERE HE IS!

COP: Settle down, goddammit!
They grab DR. CHAPMAN, *forcing him to the floor.*

DR. CHAPMAN: We can call him. He'll tell us! We can—

DOORMAN: Liar! You're lying! How can we call him?
> EDDIE *sits on the chair at* DR. CHAPMAN'*s table, as the
> police drag* DR. CHAPMAN *upstage.*

DR. CHAPMAN (*fighting, desperate*): Just telephone. THE HOS-
PITAL! I'm not going. I refuse to go with you. Just—call
the hospital.
> *The phone starts to ring.*

DR. CHAPMAN: THERE! That's him! He's calling! He's calling us!

DETECTIVE: You're making matters worse here, dammit.

COP: We'll hog-tie you if we have to.

DR. CHAPMAN (*fighting to break free*): But he wants to talk to
you—he wants to tell you! He's calling! It's him. JUST
ANSWER! ANSWER! ANSWER!
> DR. CHAPMAN *breaks free and runs to the phone.* COPS
> *and the* DOORMAN *exit as the light focuses on the table
> and telephone.* DR. CHAPMAN *grabs it up.*

DR. CHAPMAN: Hello.
> *On the screen is projected: FEBRUARY 14, 1990.*
> THOMAS *stands in a pool of light on the stage left
> apron, a phone to his ear.*

THOMAS: He's dead. Dr. Chapman, Anthony's dead. He's dead.
He died in his sleep. They called me, and I came over
immediately. I'm at the hospital now. I wasn't with him.
I—he—

Silence. THOMAS *hangs up and disappears in the dark.*
DR. CHAPMAN *hangs up. Then* DR. CHAPMAN *turns and looks up at the curtain closed around* ANTHONY.

DR. CHAPMAN: Ambroise Paré is often called the "father" of surgery. In the sixteenth century he accompanied the armies of France on their military campaigns, and in those killing fields he found an abundant resource for the education of his knife. Shattered limbs were plentiful. Wounds of every kind. Men maimed beyond hope and so docile before his desperate struggle to learn.
Music starts: the Pablo Casals recording of the 2nd Canon on the First Eight Bass Notes of the Aria Ground from Bach's "Goldberg" Variations once again. Variations 1, 2, 3, and 4.

DR. CHAPMAN: In the midst of the smoke and noise of battle, he entered a barn and found himself facing the bodies of four dead soldiers and three more who were still alive, their faces contorted with pain, their clothes still stinking and smoldering with the gunpowder that had exploded and burned them. In the pages of Paré's memoirs, he describes how there stood among them one old soldier. As Paré gazed at the wounded, writhing men with pity, the old soldier approached and asked whether there was any way to cure them. Paré shook his head no, and the old soldier turned and, in Paré's words, went up to the men and cut their throats "gently, efficiently, and without ill will." Paré cried out to the man that he was a villain. "No," said the man. "I pray God that if ever I come to be in that condition, someone will do the same for me." Villainy. Mercy. I see them now like two snakes coiled around a staff, their tangled shapes indistinguishable, their eyes fixed on each other. [*Slight pause.*] I ran into Thomas on the street once. It wasn't long after. It was an accidental encounter brought about by errands that had no relationship, but simply put us on streets that intersected. Who could have orchestrated such an encounter? Can you imagine such a mind?

THOMAS *appears on the stage left side, bundled in a coat. Head bowed, he moves across the stage toward* DR. CHAPMAN, *who walks in the opposite direction. They pass each other, and then* THOMAS *startles, whirls.*

THOMAS: Dr. Chapman.

DR. CHAPMAN *stops; they face each other.*

DR. CHAPMAN: Thomas . . . hello. How are you?

THOMAS: I'm late. But we must get together.

DR. CHAPMAN: By all means. We should talk.

THOMAS: Yes. We should talk.

THOMAS *turns and goes off.* DR. CHAPMAN *faces out. The music still plays.*

DR. CHAPMAN: Of course we didn't want to see each other. What lay between us—the secrets were better left denied. Some were his alone, of course. But there is one that belongs only to me.

A phone begins to ring.

DR. CHAPMAN: It's a thought I sometimes have, and the relief that it brings when I imagine it real fills me with shame. It's a wish, really, a wish that on that first day, when I heard that ringing telephone, I had not picked it up—I had simply let it go unanswered.

DR. CHAPMAN *turns and walks offstage left. As the phone continues to ring, the music plays. The curtain around* ANTHONY's *bed glows, as if burning from within. The phone stops, the light brightens and brightens, and then the music ends.*

The lights fade to black.

END OF PLAY